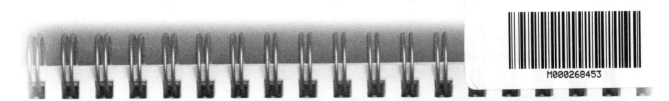

# Interactive Notebooks
# WORD STUDY

## Kindergarten

**Credits**
Content Editors: Elise Craver, Angela Triplett

Visit *carsondellosa.com* for correlations to Common Core, state, national, and Canadian provincial standards.

Carson-Dellosa Publishing LLC
PO Box 35665
Greensboro, NC 27425 USA
carsondellosa.com

© 2017, Carson-Dellosa Publishing LLC. The purchase of this material entitles the buyer to reproduce worksheets and activities for classroom use only—not for commercial resale. Reproduction of these materials for an entire school or district is prohibited. No part of this book may be reproduced (except as noted above), stored in a retrieval system, or transmitted in any form or by any means (mechanically, electronically, recording, etc.) without the prior written consent of Carson-Dellosa Publishing LLC.

Printed in the USA • All rights reserved.

978-1-4838-3808-3
02-316187784

# Table of Contents

*These lessons include multiple reproducible pages. They are designed to introduce one or more concepts at a time, and can be taught over time. Once assembled, they will use multiple pages in a student's interactive notebook.

© Carson-Dellosa • CD-104946

# What Are Interactive Notebooks?

Interactive notebooks are a unique form of note taking. Teachers guide students through creating pages of notes on new topics. Instead of being in the traditional linear, handwritten format, notes are colorful and spread across the pages. Notes also often include drawings, diagrams, and 3-D elements to make the material understandable and relevant. Students are encouraged to complete their notebook pages in ways that make sense to them. With this personalization, no two pages are exactly the same.

Because of their creative nature, interactive notebooks allow students to be active participants in their own learning. Teachers can easily differentiate pages to address the levels and needs of each learner. The notebooks are arranged sequentially, and students can create tables of contents as they create pages, making it simple for students to use their notebooks for reference throughout the year. The interactive, easily personalized format makes interactive notebooks ideal for engaging students in learning new concepts.

Using interactive notebooks can take as much or as little time as you like. Students will initially take longer to create pages but will get faster as they become familiar with the process of creating pages. You may choose to only create a notebook page as a class at the beginning of each unit, or you may choose to create a new page for each topic within a unit. You can decide what works best for your students and schedule.

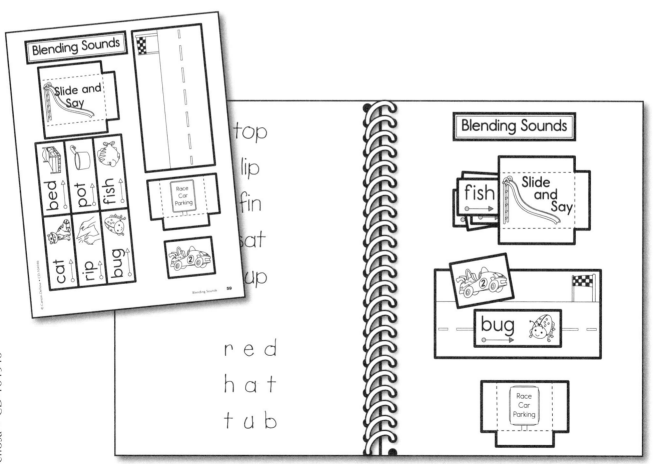

A student's interactive notebook for blending sounds

© Carson-Dellosa • CD-104946

# Getting Started

You can start using interactive notebooks at any point in the school year. Use the following guidelines to help you get started in your classroom. (For more specific details, management ideas, and tips, see page 10.)

### 1. Plan each notebook.

Use the planning template (page 9) to lay out a general plan for the topics you plan to cover in each notebook for the year.

### 2. Choose a notebook type.

Interactive notebooks are usually either single-subject, spiral-bound notebooks; composition books; or three-ring binders with loose-leaf paper. Each type presents pros and cons. See page 5 for a more in-depth look at each type of notebook.

### 3. Allow students to personalize their notebooks.

Have students decorate their notebook covers, as well as add their names and subjects. This provides a sense of ownership and emphasizes the personalized nature of the notebooks.

### 4. Number the pages and create the table of contents.

Have students number the bottom outside corner of each page, front and back. When completing a new page, adding a table of contents entry will be easy. Have students title the first page of each notebook "Table of Contents." Have them leave several blank pages at the front of each notebook for the table of contents. Refer to your general plan for an idea of about how many entries students will be creating.

### 5. Start creating pages.

Always begin a new page by adding an entry to the table of contents. Create the first notebook pages along with students to model proper format and expectations.

This book contains individual topics for you to introduce. Use the pages in the order that best fits your curriculum. You may also choose to alter the content presented to better match your school's curriculum. The provided lesson plans often do not instruct students to add color. Students should make their own choices about personalizing the content in ways that make sense to them. Encourage students to highlight and color the pages as they desire while creating them.

After introducing topics, you may choose to add more practice pages. Use the reproducibles (pages 78–96) to easily create new notebook pages for practice or to introduce topics not addressed in this book.

Use the grading rubric (page 11) to grade students' interactive notebooks at various points throughout the year. Provide students with copies of the rubric to glue into their notebooks and refer to as they create pages.

© Carson-Dellosa • CD-104946

# What Type of Notebook Should I Use?

## Spiral Notebook

*The pages in this book are formatted for a standard one-subject notebook.*

**Pros**

- Notebook can be folded in half.
- Page size is larger.
- It is inexpensive.
- It often comes with pockets for storing materials.

**Cons**

- Pages can easily fall out.
- Spirals can snag or become misshapen.
- Page count and size vary widely.
- It is not as durable as a binder.

**Tips**

- Encase the spiral in duct tape to make it more durable.
- Keep the notebooks in a central place to prevent them from getting damaged in desks.

---

## Composition Notebook

**Pros**

- Pages don't easily fall out.
- Page size and page count are standard.
- It is inexpensive.

**Cons**

- Notebook cannot be folded in half.
- Page size is smaller.
- It is not as durable as a binder.

**Tips**

- Copy pages meant for standard-sized notebooks at 85 or 90 percent. Test to see which works better for your notebook.

---

## Binder with Loose-Leaf Paper

**Pros**

- Pages can be easily added, moved, or removed.
- Pages can be removed individually for grading.
- You can add full-page printed handouts.
- It has durable covers.

**Cons**

- Pages can easily fall out.
- Pages aren't durable.
- It is more expensive than a notebook.
- Students can easily misplace or lose pages.
- Larger size makes it more difficult to store.

**Tips**

- Provide hole reinforcers for damaged pages.

© Carson-Dellosa • CD-104946

# How to Organize an Interactive Notebook

You may organize an interactive notebook in many different ways. You may choose to organize it by unit and work sequentially through the book. Or, you may choose to create different sections that you will revisit and add to throughout the year. Choose the format that works best for your students and subject.

An interactive notebook includes different types of pages in addition to the pages students create. Non-content pages you may want to add include the following:

## Title Page

This page is useful for quickly identifying notebooks. It is especially helpful in classrooms that use multiple interactive notebooks for different subjects. Have students write the subject (such as "Word Study") on the title page of each interactive notebook. They should also include their full names. You may choose to have them include other information such as the teacher's name, classroom number, or class period.

## Table of Contents

The table of contents is an integral part of the interactive notebook. It makes referencing previously created pages quick and easy for students. Make sure that students leave several pages at the beginning of each notebook for a table of contents.

## Expectations and Grading Rubric

It is helpful for each student to have a copy of the expectations for creating interactive notebook pages. You may choose to include a list of expectations for parents and students to sign, as well as a grading rubric (page 11).

## Unit Title Pages

Consider using a single page at the beginning of each section to separate it. Title the page with the unit name. Add a tab (page 78) to the edge of the page to make it easy to flip to the unit. Add a table of contents for only the pages in that unit.

## Glossary

Reserve a six-page section at the back of the notebook where students can create a glossary. Draw a line to split in half the front and back of each page, creating 24 sections. Combine Q and R and Y and Z to fit the entire alphabet. Have students add an entry as each new vocabulary word is introduced.

© Carson-Dellosa • CD-104946

# Formatting Student Notebook Pages

The other major consideration for planning an interactive notebook is how to treat the left and right sides of a notebook spread. Interactive journals are usually viewed with the notebook open flat. This creates a left side and a right side. You have several options for how to treat the two sides of the spread.

Traditionally, the right side is used for the teacher-directed part of the lesson, and the left side is used for students to interact with the lesson content. The lessons in this book use this format. However, you may prefer to switch the order for your class so that the teacher-directed learning is on the left and the student input is on the right.

It can also be important to include standards, learning objectives, or essential questions in interactive notebooks. You may choose to write these on the top-left side of each page before completing the teacher-directed page on the right side. You may also choose to have students include the "Introduction" part of each lesson in that same top-left section. This is the *in, through, out* method. Students enter *in* the lesson on the top left of the page, go *through* the lesson on the right page, and exit *out* of the lesson on the bottom left with a reflection activity.

The following chart details different types of items and activities that you could include on each side.

| Left Side<br>Student Output | Right Side<br>Teacher-Directed Learning |
| --- | --- |
| • learning objectives | • vocabulary and definitions |
| • essential questions | • mini-lessons |
| • I Can statements | • folding activities |
| • brainstorming | • steps in a process |
| • making connections | • example problems |
| • summarizing | • notes |
| • making conclusions | • diagrams |
| • practice problems | • graphic organizers |
| • opinions | • hints and tips |
| • questions | • big ideas |
| • mnemonics | |
| • drawings and diagrams | |

© Carson-Dellosa • CD-104946

# Planning for the Year

Making a general plan for interactive notebooks will help with planning, grading, and testing throughout the year. You do not need to plan every single page, but knowing what topics you will cover and in what order can be helpful in many ways.

Use the Interactive Notebook Plan (page 9) to plan your units and topics and where they should be placed in the notebooks. Remember to include enough pages at the beginning for the non-content pages, such as the title page, table of contents, and grading rubric. You may also want to leave a page at the beginning of each unit to place a mini table of contents for just that section.

In addition, when planning new pages, it can be helpful to sketch the pieces you will need to create. Use the following notebook template and notes to plan new pages.

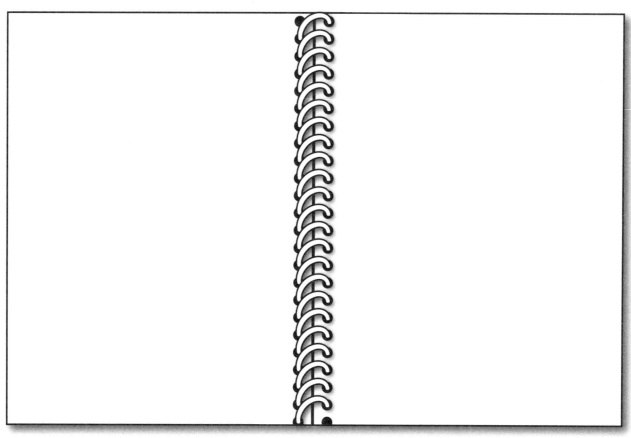

**Left Side**                                    **Right Side**

**Notes**

_____

_____

_____

© Carson-Dellosa • CD-104946

# Interactive Notebook Plan

| Page | Topic | Page | Topic |
|---|---|---|---|
| 1 | | 51 | |
| 2 | | 52 | |
| 3 | | 53 | |
| 4 | | 54 | |
| 5 | | 55 | |
| 6 | | 56 | |
| 7 | | 57 | |
| 8 | | 58 | |
| 9 | | 59 | |
| 10 | | 60 | |
| 11 | | 61 | |
| 12 | | 62 | |
| 13 | | 63 | |
| 14 | | 64 | |
| 15 | | 65 | |
| 16 | | 66 | |
| 17 | | 67 | |
| 18 | | 68 | |
| 19 | | 69 | |
| 20 | | 70 | |
| 21 | | 71 | |
| 22 | | 72 | |
| 23 | | 73 | |
| 24 | | 74 | |
| 25 | | 75 | |
| 26 | | 76 | |
| 27 | | 77 | |
| 28 | | 78 | |
| 29 | | 79 | |
| 30 | | 80 | |
| 31 | | 81 | |
| 32 | | 82 | |
| 33 | | 83 | |
| 34 | | 84 | |
| 35 | | 85 | |
| 36 | | 86 | |
| 37 | | 87 | |
| 38 | | 88 | |
| 39 | | 89 | |
| 40 | | 90 | |
| 41 | | 91 | |
| 42 | | 92 | |
| 43 | | 93 | |
| 44 | | 94 | |
| 45 | | 95 | |
| 46 | | 96 | |
| 47 | | 97 | |
| 48 | | 98 | |
| 49 | | 99 | |
| 50 | | 100 | |

© Carson-Dellosa • CD-104946

# Managing Interactive Notebooks in the Classroom

## Working with Younger Students

- Use your yearly plan to preprogram a table of contents that you can copy and give to students to glue into their notebooks, instead of writing individual entries.

- Have assistants or parent volunteers precut pieces.

- Create glue sponges to make gluing easier. Place large sponges in plastic containers with white glue. The sponges will absorb the glue. Students can wipe the backs of pieces across the sponges to apply the glue with less mess.

## Creating Notebook Pages

- For storing loose pieces, add a pocket to the inside back cover. Use the envelope pattern (page 81), an envelope, a jumbo library pocket, or a resealable plastic bag. Or, tape the bottom and side edges of the two last pages of the notebook together to create a large pocket.

- When writing under flaps, have students trace the outline of each flap so that they can visualize the writing boundary.

- Where the dashed line will be hidden on the inside of the fold, have students first fold the piece in the opposite direction so that they can see the dashed line. Then, students should fold the piece back the other way along the same fold line to create the fold in the correct direction.

- To avoid losing pieces, have students keep all of their scraps on their desks until they have finished each page.

- To contain paper scraps and avoid multiple trips to the trash can, provide small groups with small buckets or tubs.

- For students who run out of room, keep full and half sheets available. Students can glue these to the bottom of the pages and fold them up when not in use.

## Dealing with Absences

- Create a model notebook for absent students to reference when they return to school.

- Have students cut a second set of pieces as they work on their own pages.

## Using the Notebook

- To organize sections of the notebook, provide each student with a sheet of tabs (page 78).

- To easily find the next blank page, either cut off the top-right corner of each page as it is used or attach a long piece of yarn or ribbon to the back cover to be used as a bookmark.

© Carson-Dellosa • CD-104946

# Interactive Notebook Grading Rubric

**4**

_____ Table of contents is complete.

_____ All notebook pages are included.

_____ All notebook pages are complete.

_____ Notebook pages are neat and organized.

_____ Information is correct.

_____ Pages show personalization, evidence of learning, and original ideas.

**3**

_____ Table of contents is mostly complete.

_____ One notebook page is missing.

_____ Notebook pages are mostly complete.

_____ Notebook pages are mostly neat and organized.

_____ Information is mostly correct.

_____ Pages show some personalization, evidence of learning, and original ideas.

**2**

_____ Table of contents is missing a few entries.

_____ A few notebook pages are missing.

_____ A few notebook pages are incomplete.

_____ Notebook pages are somewhat messy and unorganized.

_____ Information has several errors.

_____ Pages show little personalization, evidence of learning, or original ideas.

**1**

_____ Table of contents is incomplete.

_____ Many notebook pages are missing.

_____ Many notebook pages are incomplete.

_____ Notebook pages are too messy and unorganized to use.

_____ Information is incorrect.

_____ Pages show no personalization, evidence of learning, or original ideas.

© Carson-Dellosa • CD-104946

# Sight Words

## Introduction

Before beginning instruction with sight words, each student should be able to identify all of the lowercase letters easily. Provide each student with a page that has all of the lowercase letters listed. Say letters and have students see how fast they can find them on their page. Then, write simple words on the board and have students identify the letters. Explain that letters are building blocks and that they can be put together in many ways to create different words.

## Creating the Notebook Page

Guide students through the following steps to complete the right-hand page in their notebooks.

1. Add a Table of Contents entry for the Sight Words pages.

2. Cut out the title (the sight word in the word shape box) and glue it to the top of the page.

3. Discuss the shape of the sight word in the title. Then, say each letter from left to right and color each letter.

4. Cut out the letter tiles and glue them in the correct order below and to the left of the title. Trace each letter in order on the letter tiles. Then, write the word on the page below the tiles.

5. Cut out the *Unscramble the letters.* flap book. Cut on the solid line or lines to create two or three flaps. Apply glue to the back of the left section and attach it to the page beside the letter tiles. Under each flap, write the unscrambled sight word.

6. Cut out the three large flaps. Apply glue to the gray glue sections at the top of two flaps and stack all three flaps to create a stacked three-flap book. Glue the flap book to the bottom of the page. Complete the activity on each flap.

7. Use the blank template on page 21 to create pages for sight words of your choosing. Use the light grid on the title piece to help create the word shape box. Have students discard any unused letter tiles.

## Reflect on Learning

To complete the left-hand page, have students practice using and writing the sight word in a variety of ways. For example, have students use letter stamps, cut out and glue down letters cut from magazines, or write the letters with a variety of fun writing utensils. Or, provide students with copies of several short sentences that contain the sight word to glue in their notebooks. Then, have students highlight the sight word in each sentence.

© Carson-Dellosa • CD-104946

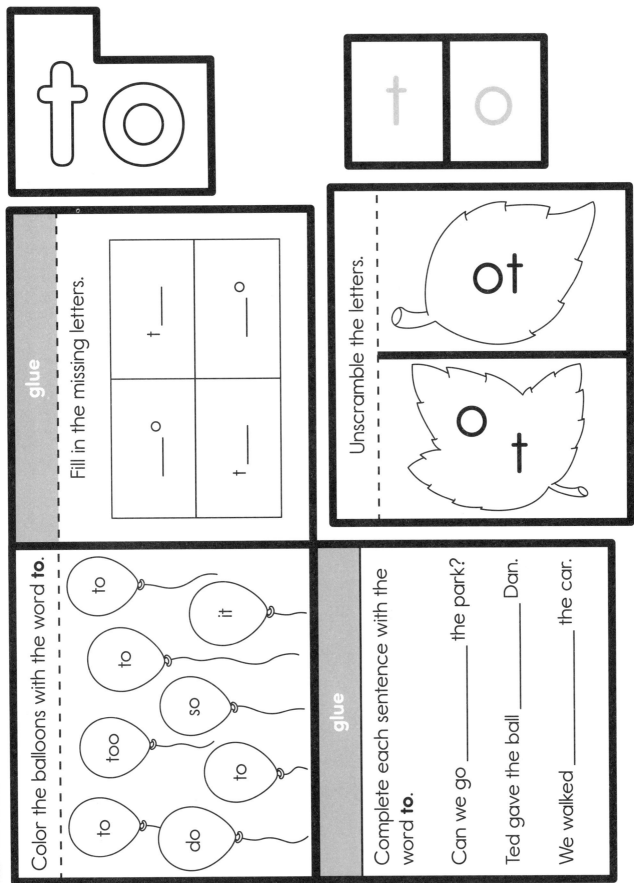

**to**

Fill in the missing letters.

glue

Unscramble the letters.

ot

o t

Color the balloons with the word **to.**

to  it  to  so  too  to  to  do

Complete each sentence with the word **to.**

Can we go _____ the park?

Ted gave the ball _____ Dan.

We walked _____ the car.

glue

© Carson-Dellosa • CD-104946

**is**

i  s

Fill in the missing letters.

| i | ___ s |
|---|---|
| ___ s | i ___ |

glue

Unscramble the letters.

s  i

s  i

Color the stars with the word **is**.

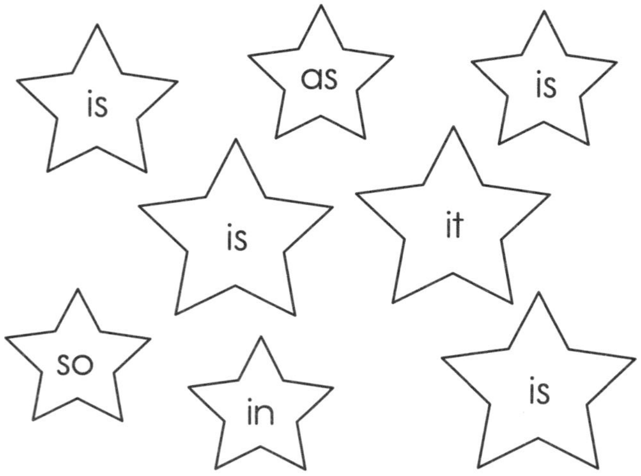

is

it

is

as

is

in

is

so

Complete each sentence with the word **is**.

glue

_____ it time for lunch?

Riding a bike _____ fun!

Your dress _____ very pretty.

© Carson-Dellosa • CD-104946

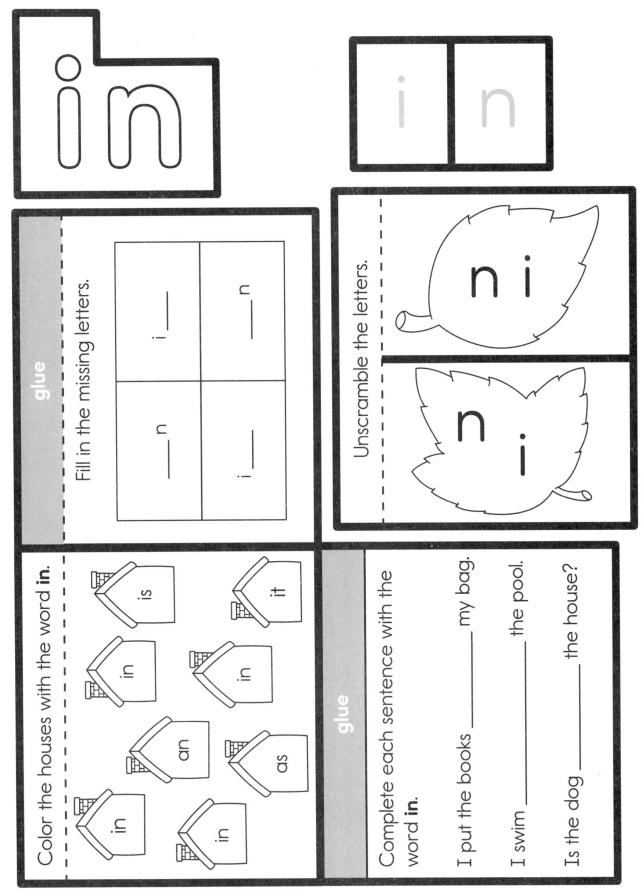

in

i | n

© Carson-Dellosa • CD-104946

**glue**

Fill in the missing letters.

| i _ | _ n |
|-----|-----|
| _ n | i _ |

Unscramble the letters.

n i

n

i

Color the houses with the word **in**.

is

it

in

in

an

as

in

in

**glue**

Complete each sentence with the word **in**.

I put the books _____ my bag.

I swim _____ the pool.

Is the dog _____ the house?

of

o | f

## Fill in the missing letters.

| f ___ | ___ o |
|-------|-------|
| ___ f | o ___ |

glue

## Unscramble the letters.

f o

f o

## Color the cupcakes with the word **of**.

to

of

if

of

on

so

of

of

## Complete each sentence with the word **of**.

All _____ my friends are kind.

This is one _____ the best toys.

I know all _____ my sight words!

glue

© Carson-Dellosa • CD-104946

# the

t h e

## Fill in the missing letters.

| __ he | t __ e |
|-------|--------|
| th __ | __ h __ |

## Unscramble the letters.

h e t

e t h

t e h

**glue**

## Color the apples with the word **the**.

the · he · the · the · her · with · the · the

**glue**

## Complete each sentence with the word **the**.

Where did _____ ball go?

You can eat _____ candy later.

I like _____ dog best!

© Carson-Dellosa • CD-104946

# and

| a | n | d |

**Fill in the missing letters.**

| an ___ | ___ nd |
| n ___ | a ___ d |

**Unscramble the letters.**

d n a

n a d

d a n

**Color the books with the word and.**

| all | and |
| ant | ate |
| and | and |
| and | and |

**Complete each sentence with the word and.**

My mom _____ I are going to the park.

I like pizza _____ hot dogs.

My bike is red _____ white.

© Carson-Dellosa • CD-104946

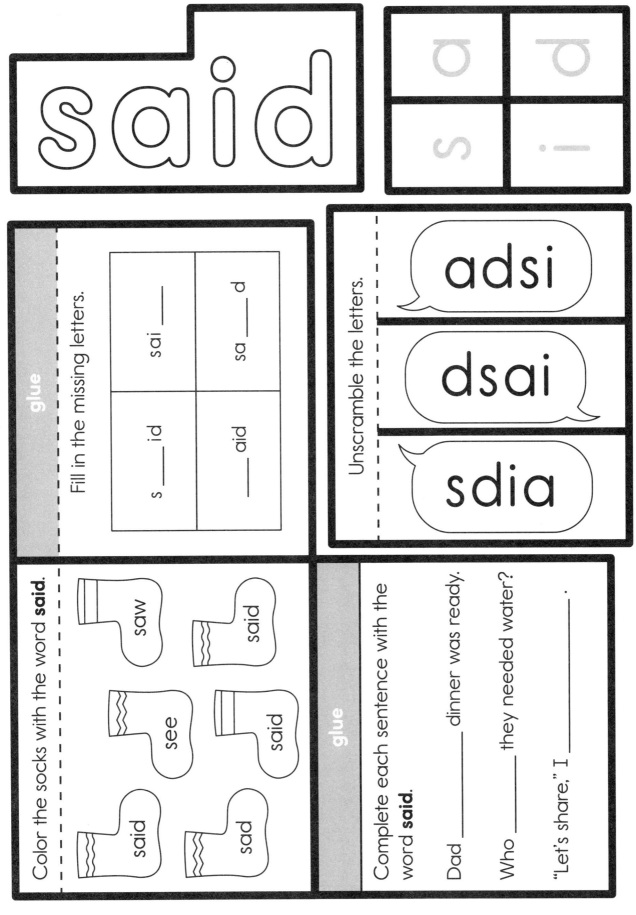

said

a    d

s    i

Fill in the missing letters.

| sai ___ | s ___ id |
| sa ___ d | ___ aid |

Unscramble the letters.

adsi

dsai

sdia

glue

Color the socks with the word **said.**

saw

see

said

said

said

sad

glue

Complete each sentence with the word **said.**

Dad ___ dinner was ready.

Who ___ they needed water?

"Let's share," I ___ .

© Carson-Dellosa • CD-104946

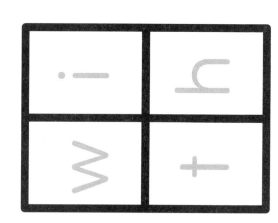

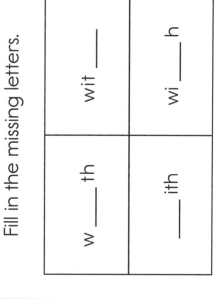

Fill in the missing letters.

glue

| w ___ th | wit ___ |
| ___ ith | wi ___ h |

Unscramble the letters.

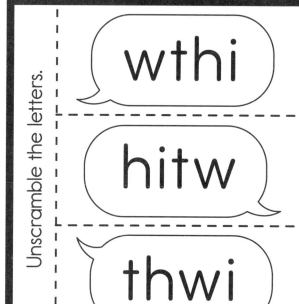

wthi

hitw

thwi

Color the flowers with the word **with**.

Complete each sentence with the word **with**.

I walk to school _____ my friend.

Do you want milk _____ that?

I like pizza _____ cheese.

glue

© Carson-Dellosa • CD-104946

© Carson-Dellosa • CD-104946

**glue**

Fill in the missing letters.

Unscramble the letters.

Color the balls with the word _____.

**glue**

Complete each sentence with the word _____.

# Letter Sounds

*Note: Only consonants are covered in this lesson. Long and short vowels are covered on pages 34–47.*

## Introduction

Display a simple tongue twister or alliterative phrase on the board, such as *Many monsters make mud pies* or *Bob bought better butter.* Say it aloud several times, pointing to each word as you say it. Have students identify the similar sound in the tongue twister. As a class, discuss how the same letter repeats, so you hear the same sound over and over. Explain that letters have their own sounds, which can help you read words.

## Creating the Notebook Page

Guide students through the following steps to complete the right-hand page in their notebooks.

1. Add a Table of Contents entry for the Letter Sounds pages.

2. Cut out the title (the upper- and lowercase letters piece) and glue it to the top of the page.

3. Color in the uppercase and lowercase letter. Discuss both forms and the sound the letter makes.

4. Cut out the six flaps. Say the name of the object on each flap. Discard the flap that does not have the correct sound. Apply glue to the back of the top section of each remaining flap and attach it to the page.

5. Cut out the five word cards. Glue each card under the matching flap. It may be helpful to cut off one word at a time to provide guidance to beginning readers.

6. Look at the word under each flap and identify the letter(s) that makes the focus sound. Circle, color, or highlight the letter(s) on each word card.

7. Use any extra space on the page to write or draw more words that start with the focus sound.

8. Use the blank template on page 23 to create additional pages for letter sounds, such as long and short vowels or soft and hard *c* or *g*.

## Reflect on Learning

To complete the left-hand page, provide students with a set of pictures to glue in their notebook. Most pictures should start with the target sound, but some should not. Have students say the name of each picture and draw an *X* on the pictures that do not start with the target sound.

© Carson-Dellosa • CD-104645

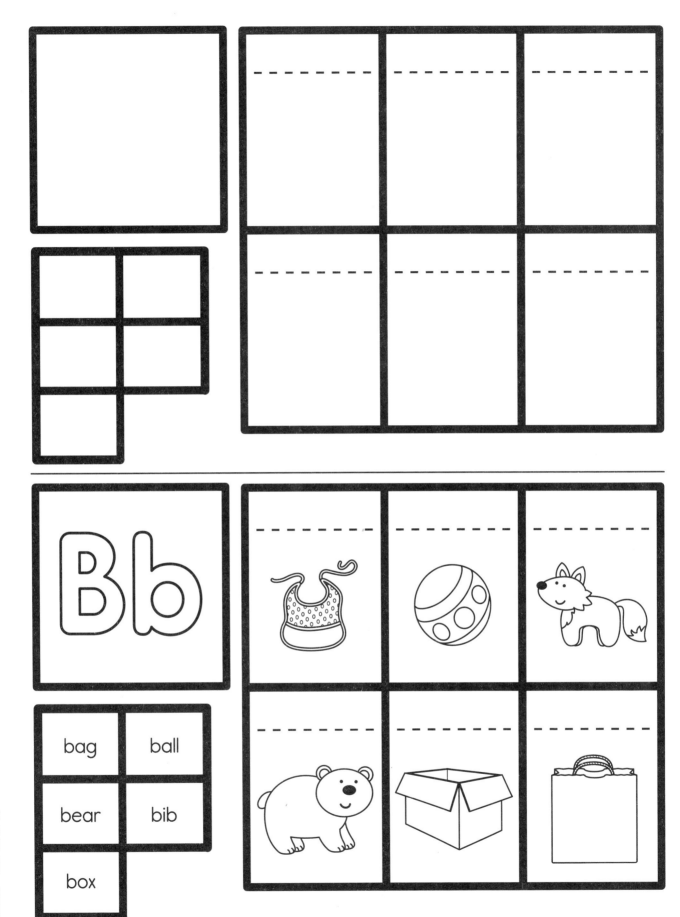

bag    ball

bear    bib

box

© Carson-Dellosa • CD-104946

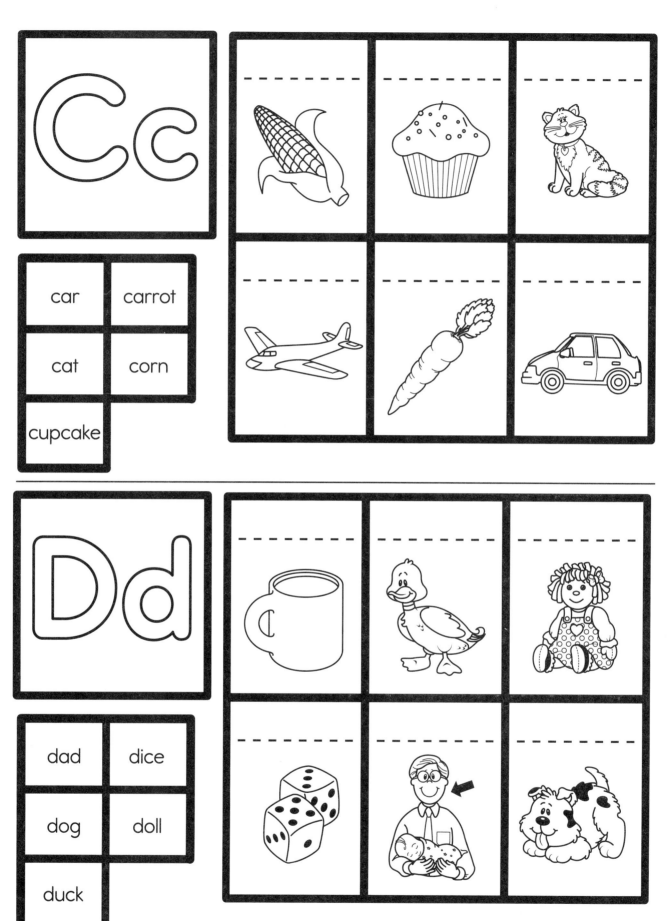

# Cc

| car | carrot |
|-----|--------|
| cat | corn |
| cupcake | |

# Dd

| dad | dice |
|-----|------|
| dog | doll |
| duck | |

© Carson-Dellosa • CD-104946

# Ff

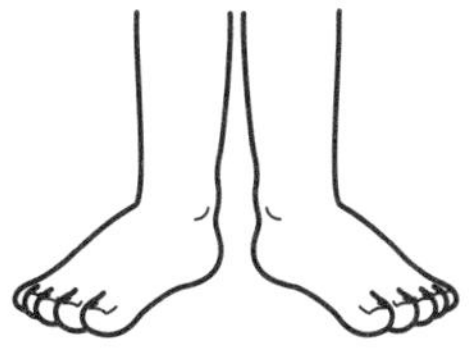

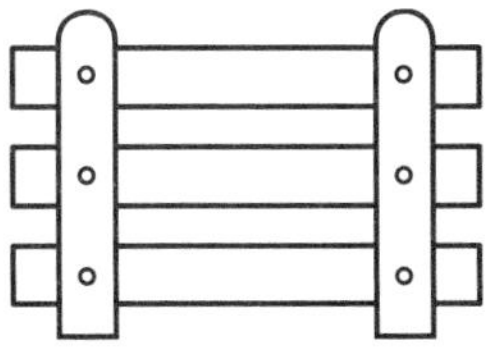

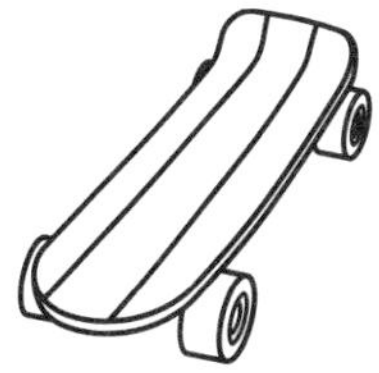

five | feet
fox | fence
fish

# Gg

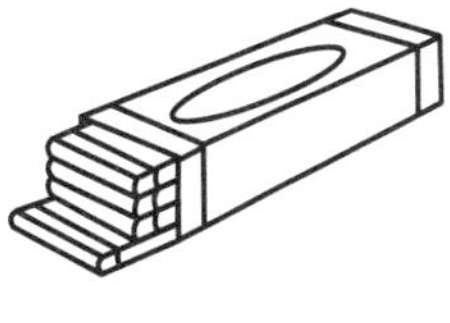

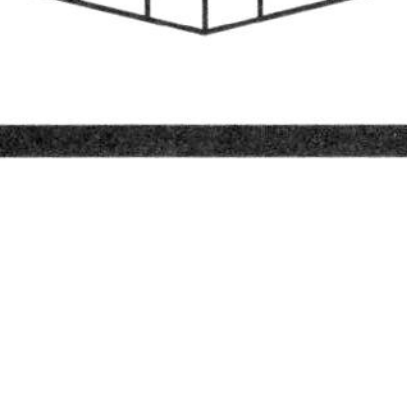

goat | gum
game | gift
girl

© Carson-Dellosa • CD-104946

# H h

| house | hat |
|-------|-----|
| hand | heart |
| horse | |

# J j

| jet | jug |
|------|------|
| juice | jump |
| jacket | |

© Carson-Dellosa • CD-104946

# Kk

king | kitten
key | kite
kangaroo

# Ll

leaf | log
lock | lion
lamp

© Carson-Dellosa • CD-104946

# M m

mouse | mitten
man | mop
moon

# N n

nut | nail
nine | net
nest

© Carson-Dellosa • CD-104946

# Pp

pan    pear
pie    paint
pumpkin

# Qq

quack    quiet
quilt    queen
quail

© Carson-Dellosa • CD-104946

**R r**

rake | road
rope | rug
rose

**S s**

7

soap | sun
seven | seed
seal

© Carson-Dellosa • CD-104946

## T t

| two | table |
|-----|-------|
| tire | tent |
| turtle | |

## V v

| vase | van |
|------|-----|
| violin | vine |
| vest | |

© Carson-Dellosa • CD-104946

## Ww

| web | window |
|-----|--------|
| wagon | wing |
| wig | |

## Xx

| fox | box |
|-----|-----|
| six | X-ray |
| ox | |

© Carson-Dellosa • CD-104946

# Yy

yak   yarn

yawn   yo-yo

yogurt

5

# Zz

zoo   puzzle

zipper   zebra

pizza

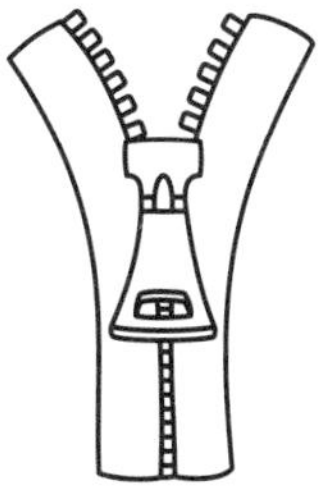

© Carson-Dellosa • CD-104946

# Short Vowels

## Introduction

Review consonant sounds with a quick whole-class game. Before the lesson, write one word or glue a picture for each consonant on an index card or self-stick note. Write the entire alphabet on the board, leaving space below each letter. Give each student one card or note, and have him place it below the correct letter. After all cards have been placed, discuss how the remaining letters are called vowels.

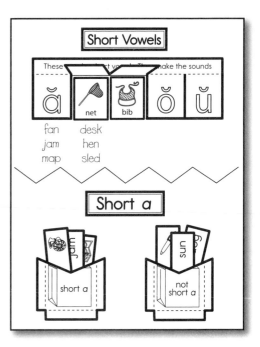

## Creating the Notebook Page

Guide students through the following steps to complete the right-hand page in their notebooks.

1. Add a Table of Contents entry for the Short Vowels pages.

2. Cut out the title and glue it to the top of the page.

3. Cut out the flap book. Cut on the solid lines to create five flaps. Apply glue to the back of the top section and attach it to the page below the title.

4. Cut out the word cards. Identify the sound each vowel makes and glue it under the matching flap. Use the space below each flap to record additional words that have each vowel sound.

5. For each vowel sound, cut out the title and glue it to the top of a new page.

6. Cut out the pockets. Apply glue to the back of the three tabs and attach the pockets to the page below the title. It may be helpful to fold on the dashed lines to create visual borders before applying the glue.

7. Cut out the picture and word cards. Say the word on each card aloud and sort it into the correct pocket. Point out the picture on the pockets and how it makes the short vowel sound too. If desired, use index cards cut in half length-wise to add more words to sort.

8. Use the remaining space on the page to create a personal dictionary for that short vowel. Return to this page throughout the year to add new words with that short vowel sound.

## Reflect on Learning

To complete the left-hand page, record several CVC words without the vowels on the board, such as c_t and m_n. Have students record the words in their notebooks and fill in the blank with the vowel they studied. Then, students should read each word and draw a picture to illustrate it.

© Carson-Dellosa • CD-104946

# Short Vowels

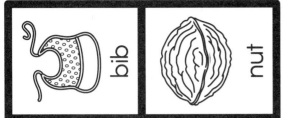

cat    pot    net

 bib     nut

These are the short vowels. They make the sounds

ă    ĕ    ĭ    ŏ    ŭ

# Short a

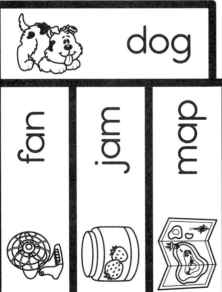

dog

fan    jam    map    pen    sun

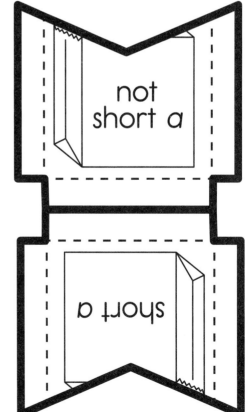

not
short a

short a

© Carson-Dellosa • CD-104946

# Short e

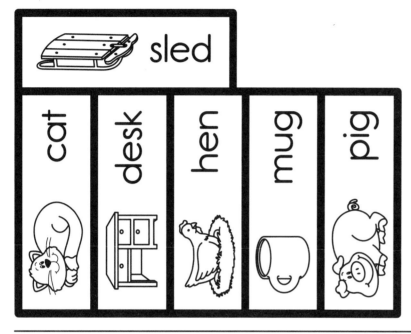

sled

cat | desk | hen | mug | pig

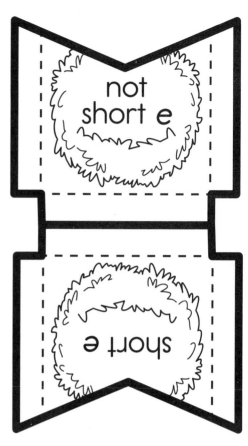

not short e

short e

---

# Short i

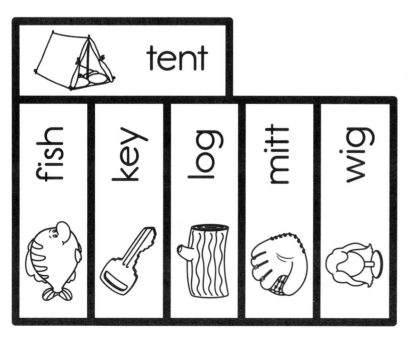

tent

fish | key | log | mitt | wig

not short i

short i

© Carson-Dellosa • CD-104946

# Short o

STOP stop

| gift | gum | lamb | log | sock |
|------|-----|------|-----|------|

not short o

short o

# Short u

top

| bed | bus | can | hut | run |
|-----|-----|-----|-----|-----|

not short u

short u

© Carson-Dellosa • CD-104946

# Long Vowels

© Carson-Dellosa • CD-104946

## Introduction

Review short vowel sounds. Before the lesson, program index cards with short vowel words or pictures. Give each student an index card and have the class move around the room and find all of the other students with the same short vowel sound. Once all groups have been formed, have each group read their words aloud. Explain that vowels can make long sounds too. When a vowel makes the long sound, it says its name.

## Creating the Notebook Page

Guide students through the following steps to complete the right-hand page in their notebooks.

1.  Add a Table of Contents entry for the Long Vowels pages.

2.  Cut out the title and glue it to the top of the page.

3.  Cut out the flap book. Cut on the solid lines to create five flaps. Apply glue to the back of the top section and attach it to the page below the title.

4.  Cut out the word cards. Identify the sound each vowel makes and glue it under the matching flap. Use the space below each flap to record additional words that have each vowel sound.

5.  For each vowel sound, cut out the title and glue it to the top of a new page.

6.  Cut out the pockets. Apply glue to the back of the three tabs and attach the pockets to the page below the title. It may be helpful to fold on the dashed lines to create visual borders before applying the glue.

7.  Cut out the picture and word cards. Say the word on each card aloud and sort it into the correct pocket. Point out the picture on the pockets and how it makes the long vowel sound too. If desired, use index cards cut in half length-wise to add more words to sort.

8.  Use the remaining space on the page to create a personal dictionary for that long vowel. Return to this page throughout the year to add new words with that long vowel sound.

## Reflect on Learning

To complete the left-hand page, provide students with several word or picture pairs to glue in their notebooks. Word pairs should emphasize the difference between the short and long vowel sounds (for example, *can/cane, bet/beet, pin/pine, hop/hope,* or *tub/tube*). Have students read each pair and circle the short vowel words in one color and circle the long vowel words in a different color.

# Long Vowels

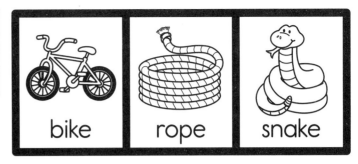

bike | rope | snake

 sheep

 tube

These are the long vowels. They say their name.

| ā | ē | ī | ō | ū |

# Long a

 boot

 cake

 deer

nine

day

plate

not long a

long a

© Carson-Dellosa • CD-104946

# Long e

cheese

goose · peach · toast · train · wheel

not long e

long e

# Long i

feet

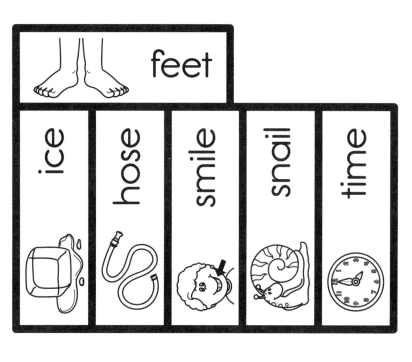

ice · hose · smile · snail · time

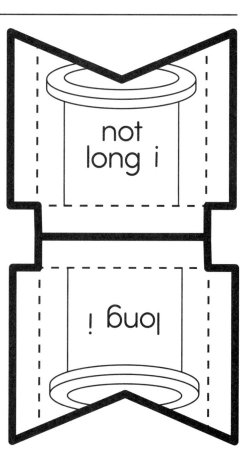

not long i

long i

© Carson-Dellosa • CD-104946

# Long o

leaf

paint  phone  nose  soap  teeth

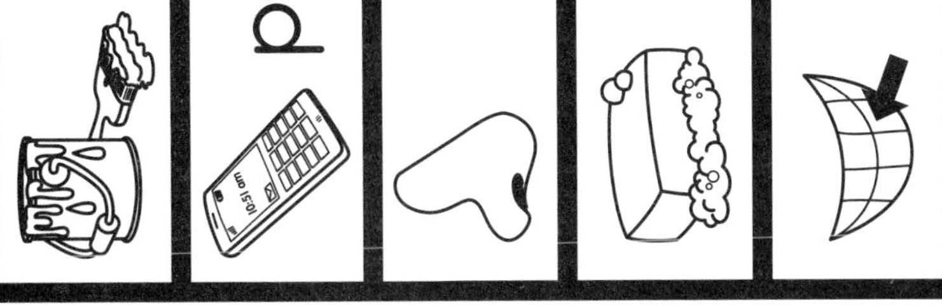

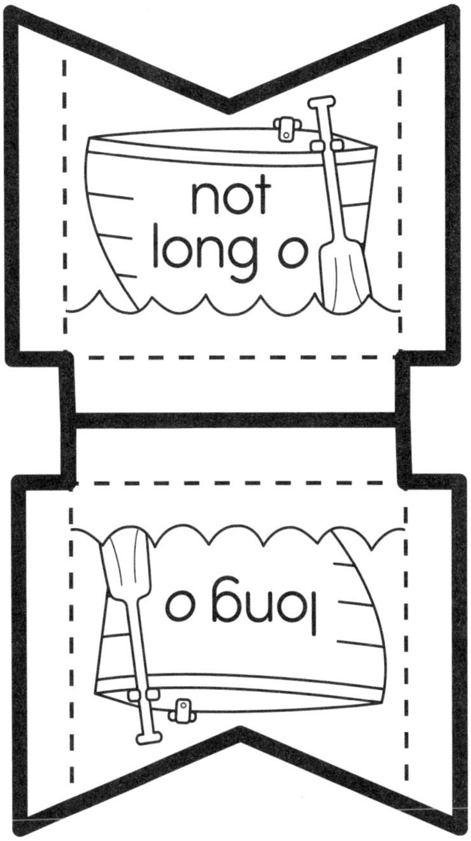

not
long o

long o

# Long u

coat

cube  glue  mice  mule  tray

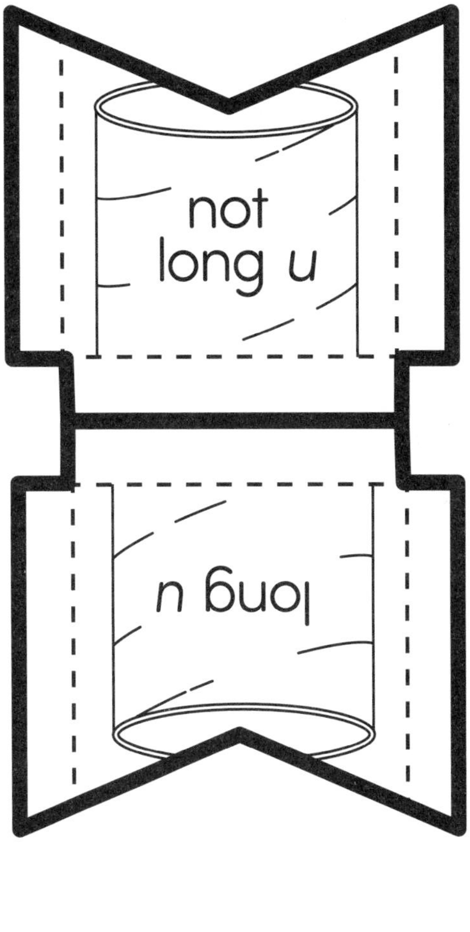

not
long u

long u

© Carson-Dellosa • CD-104946

# Short and Long Vowels

## Introduction

Review short and long vowel sounds. As a class, come up with two motions—one for short vowels and one for long vowels. For example, you may choose to hold your hands close together to symbolize short vowels and hold your arms wide open to symbolize long vowels. Say several short and long vowel words aloud and have students do the matching motion for each word. Explain that knowing the difference between short and long vowel sounds can help them read and say words.

## Creating the Notebook Page

Guide students through the following steps to complete the right-hand page in their notebooks.

1. Add a Table of Contents entry for the Short and Long Vowels pages.

2. Cut out the title and glue it to the top of the page.

3. Cut out the *short* and *long* vowel pieces. For *a*, glue one piece at the bottom of the page and one piece halfway up the page. For *e* and *u*, glue them to the page as space allows. For *i*, glue one piece below the title and the other halfway down the page. For *o*, glue them side-by-side at the bottom of the page.

4. Cut out the word and picture cards. Say each word and sort them by vowel sound. For *a* and *o*, glue them above the correct vowel sound. For *e* and *u* glue them on the correct vowel sound. For *i*, glue them below the correct vowel sound. If desired, point out how the art for each vowel is a related short and/or long vowel word (*plate* and *cupcake* for *a*, *tree* and *leaf* for *e*, *fish* for *i*, *bone* and *bowl* for *o*, and *gum* for *u*).

## Reflect on Learning

To complete the left-hand page, provide students with a short sentence or sentences to glue in their notebook. Each sentence should have a short and long vowel word or words for the vowel sound being studied (for example, *The cat ate cake.* or *I like fig pie.*). Have students circle each short vowel sound in one color and each long vowel sound in a different color. It may be helpful to read each sentence together as a class first.

© Carson-Dellosa • CD-104946

# Short and Long a

long a

short a

mask

can

cake

plate

apple

hat

bag

game

vase

tape

© Carson-Dellosa • CD-104946

# Short and Long e

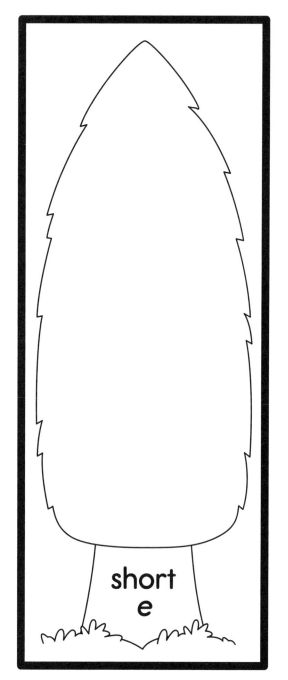

short
e

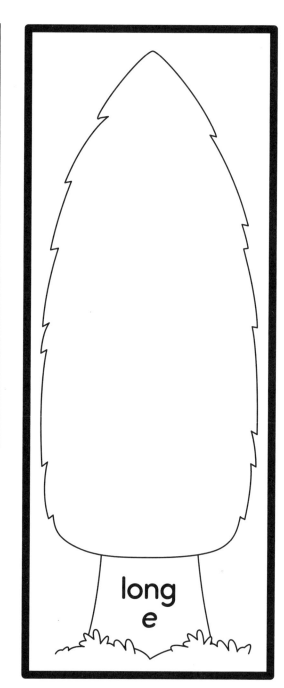

long
e

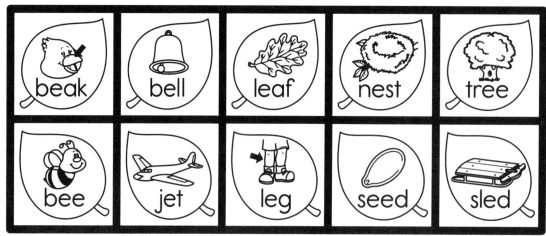

beak

bell

leaf

nest

tree

bee

jet

leg

seed

sled

© Carson-Dellosa • CD-104946

# Short and Long *i*

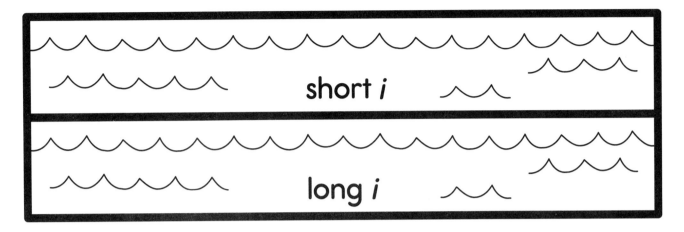

short *i*

long *i*

dive

fin

pipe

fish

5 five

swim

hill

like

lip

pie

© Carson-Dellosa • CD-104946

# Short and Long o

short o

long o

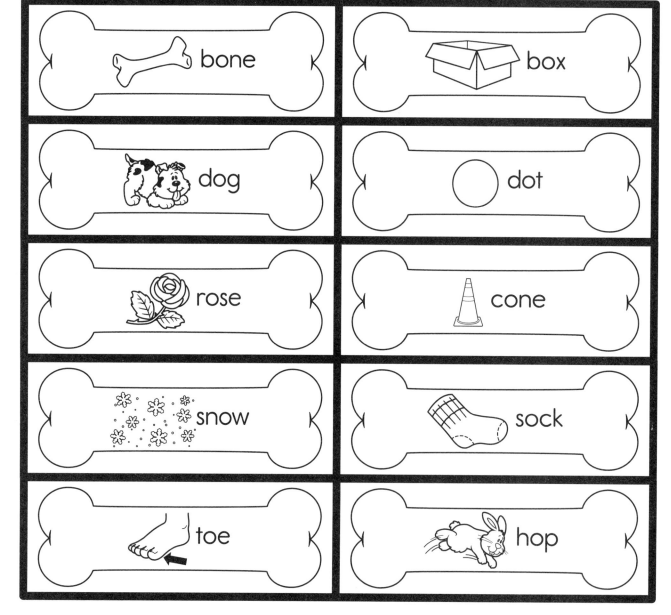

bone

box

dog

dot

rose

cone

snow

sock

toe

hop

© Carson-Dellosa • CD-104946

# Short and Long *u*

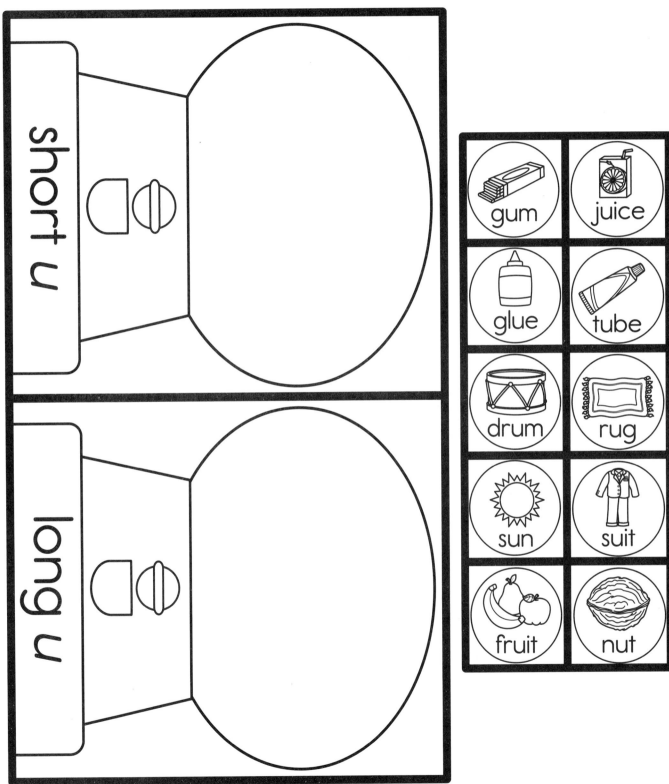

short u

long u

gum
juice
glue
tube
drum
rug
sun
suit
fruit
nut

© Carson-Dellosa • CD-104946

# Y as a Vowel

Write several words with the letter *y* on the board. Include some that use *y* as a consonant (*yarn, yo-yo*), and some that use *y* as a vowel (*fly, baby*). As a class, read each word aloud several times. Then, ask students to pay attention to the *y* in each word as they say it. It may be helpful to point to the sounds in each word as they are voiced to help students hear the different *y* sounds. Explain that *y* can make different sounds, including vowel sounds.

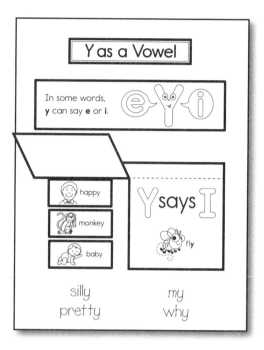

## Creating the Notebook Page

Guide students through the following steps to complete the right-hand page in their notebooks.

1. Add a Table of Contents entry for the *Y as a Vowel* pages.

2. Cut out the title and glue it to the top of the page.

3. Cut out the teaching box and glue it below the title.

4. As a class, discuss how *y* can be a vowel, and how it usually occurs when it is at the end of a word. Explain that it can make the long *e* or long *i* sound.

5. Cut out the flap book. Cut on the solid line to create two flaps. Apply glue to the back of the top section and attach it to the page below the teaching box.

6. Discuss the two sounds *y* makes and point out the example on each flap.

7. Cut out the word cards. Say each word and glue it under the correct flap. If desired, look for a pattern within each set of words. Discuss how *y* sounds like long *i* when it has one syllable (or is a "short word"), and it sounds like long *e* when it has two syllables (or is a "long word").

8. Use the space below the flap book to write more example words.

## Reflect on Learning

To complete the left-hand page, have students create a three-column chart with the headers *yo-yo*, *cry*, and *baby*. Give them several words, either by saying them aloud, writing them on the board, or providing word cards to glue in their notebook. Have students place each word in the correct column, depending on which sound the *y* makes.

© Carson-Dellosa • CD-104946

# Y as a Vowel

In some words, **y** can say **e** or **i**.

Y says E

puppy

Y says I

fly

baby  cry  happy  monkey  sky  sty

© Carson-Dellosa • CD-104946

# Recognizing Beginning, Middle, and Ending Sounds

## Introduction

Provide each student with an index card. Write a CVC word on the board. (Do not use words with a repeated letter, such as *bib* or *pop*.) Have students record it on the index card, writing it large enough to fill most of the card. Then, have students cut the word into three letters. Students should then try to reassemble the word. Have them explain how they knew which letter to place at the beginning, middle, and end.

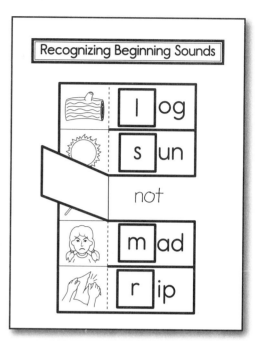

## Creating the Notebook Page

Guide students through the following steps to complete the right-hand page in their notebooks.

1. Add a Table of Contents entry for the Recognizing Beginning, Middle, and Ending Sounds pages.

2. Cut out the title and glue it to the top of the page.

3. Cut out the flap book. Cut on the solid lines to create five flaps. Apply glue to the back of the left section and attach it to the page.

4. Cut out the letter cards.

5. Look at the picture to the left of each word. Say its name. Identify the correct beginning, middle, or ending sound, and glue the matching letter in the box.

6. Under each flap, write a different word with the same beginning, middle, or ending sound.

## Reflect on Learning

To complete the left-hand page, say three words with the same beginning, middle, or ending sound. Have students record the sound they have in common. Repeat the activity several times.

© Carson-Dellosa • CD-104946

# Recognizing Beginning Sounds

© Carson-Dellosa • CD-104946

# Recognizing Middle Sounds

Recognizing Beginning, Middle, and Ending Sounds

© Carson-Dellosa • CD-104946

# Recognizing Ending Sounds

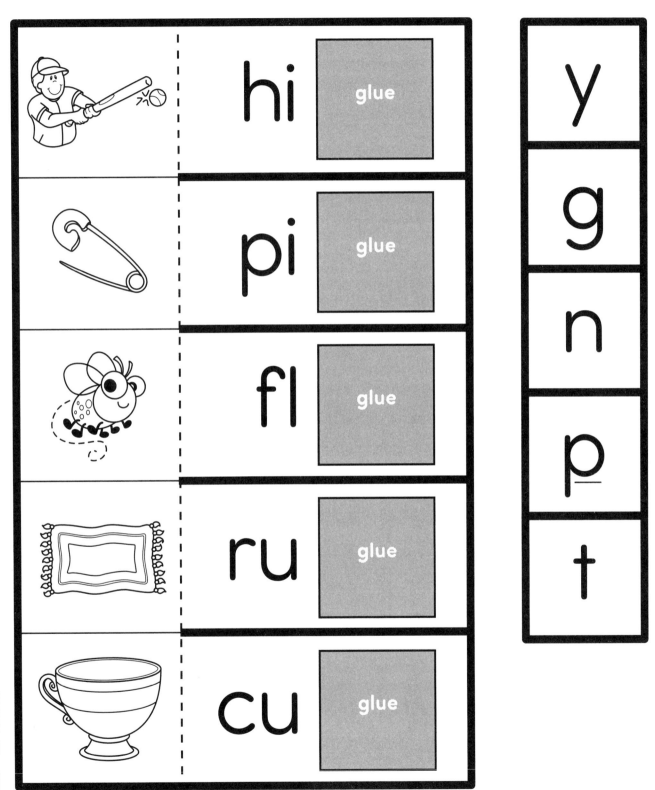

hi ___

pi ___

fl ___

ru ___

cu ___

y

g

n

p

t

© Carson-Dellosa • CD-104946

# Adding and Substituting Beginning, Middle, and Ending Sounds

## Introduction

Write two CVC words on the board whose letters can be switched to create new words, such as *pan* and *fin*, or *rug* and *bib*. Write the letters to be switched on self-stick notes so they can be easily moved. As a class, read each word. Then, switch the letters and read the new words. Explain how beginning, middle, or ending sounds can be changed to create new words.

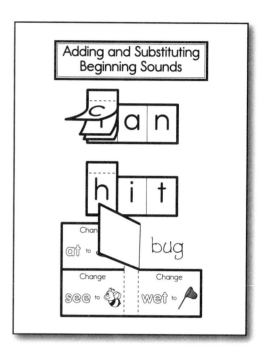

## Creating the Notebook Page

Guide students through the following steps to complete the right-hand page in their notebooks.

1. Add a Table of Contents entry for the Adding and Substituting Beginning, Middle, and Ending Sounds pages.

2. Cut out the title and glue it to the top of the page.

3. Cut out the left-hand set of pieces (a set of three flaps and a two-letter piece). Glue the two-letter piece below the title.

4. Cut apart the three flaps. Apply glue to the gray glue sections and stack the flaps to create a stacked three-flap book. Apply glue to the back of the top section and attach it to the page so it covers the blank section on the two-letter piece.

5. Repeat steps 3 and 4 with the remaining set of letter pieces. Attach it below the first set.

6. On each letter piece, raise the flaps to change the beginning, middle, or ending sound of the word. Discuss how some two-letter pieces already spell a word (*it, an, be*), so the sounds are being added to create a new word. If desired, write an additional letter in the blank space to create a fourth word.

7. Cut out the flap book. Cut on the solid lines to create four flaps. Apply glue to the back of the center section and attach it to the bottom of the page.

8. Read the riddle on each flap. Write the answer under the flap.

## Reflect on Learning

To complete the left-hand page, have students write a CVC word in their notebooks. Then, challenge students to change the beginning, middle, or ending sound to create as many new words as they can. It may be helpful to remind students to use the alphabet posted on the wall or provide them with an alphabet strip to glue in their notebooks.

© Carson-Dellosa • CD-104946

# Adding and Substituting Beginning Sounds

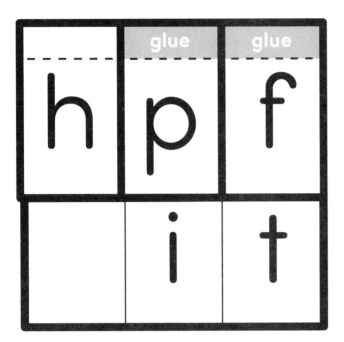

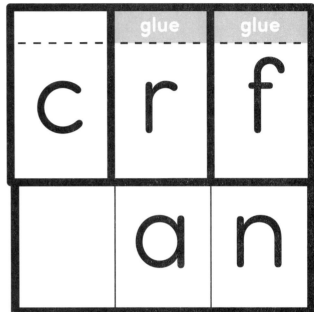

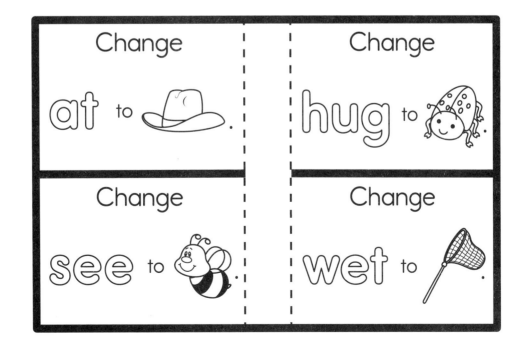

© Carson-Dellosa • CD-104946

# Adding and Substituting Middle Sounds

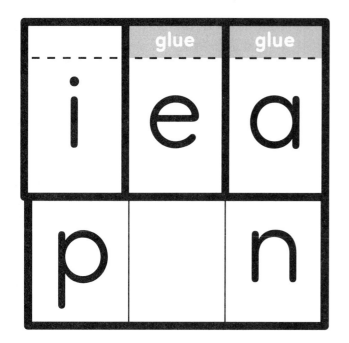

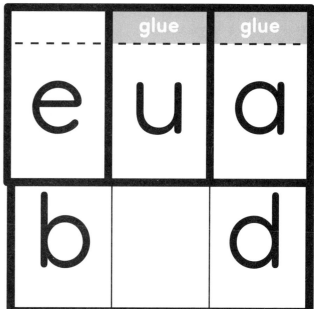

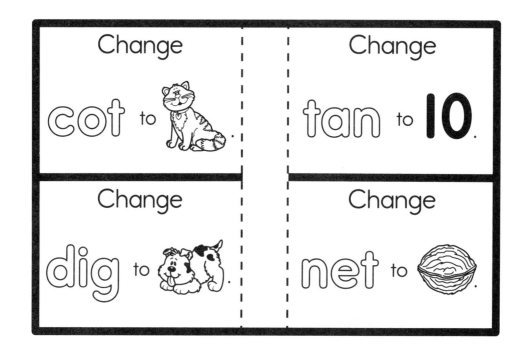

Change cot to 🐱.

Change tan to **10**.

Change dig to 🐶.

Change net to 🥥.

© Carson-Dellosa • CD-104946

# Adding and Substituting Ending Sounds

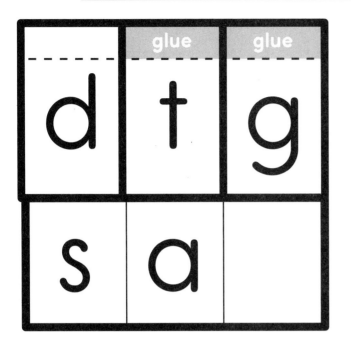

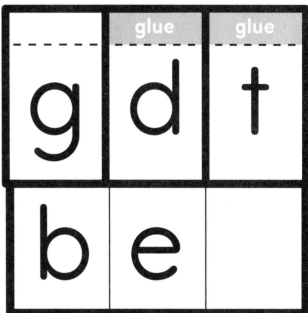

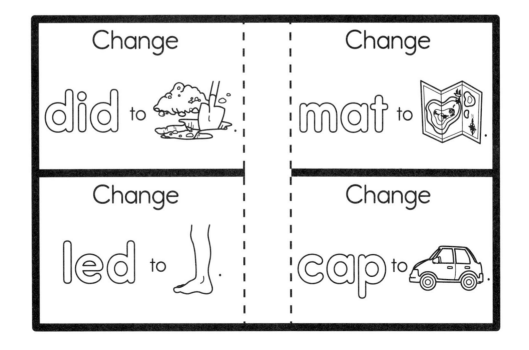

Change did to [image].

Change mat to [image].

Change led to [image].

Change cap to [image].

© Carson-Dellosa • CD-104946

# Blending Sounds

## Introduction

Write a short sentence, such as *A cat sat.* on the board. Read it aloud using the letter sounds instead of blending each word (/a/ /k/ /a/ /t/. . .). As a class, discuss how it sounded and why. Then, read the sentence normally. Explain that readers use the letter sounds, but they blend the sounds together to create words.

## Creating the Notebook Page

Guide students through the following steps to complete the right-hand page in their notebooks.

1. Add a Table of Contents entry for the Blending Sounds pages.

2. Cut out the title and glue it to the top of the page.

3. Cut out the *Slide and Say* pocket. Apply glue to the backs of the three tabs and attach the pocket to the page below the title. It may be helpful to have students fold on the dashed lines to create visual borders before applying the glue.

4. Cut out the race track piece and glue it below the pocket.

5. Cut out the *Race Car Parking* pocket. Apply glue to the backs of the three tabs and attach the pocket to the bottom of the page. It may be helpful to have students fold on the dashed lines to create visual borders before applying the glue.

6. Cut out the race car. Store it in the *Race Car Parking* pocket.

7. Cut out the word cards.

8. Color the dot on each word card green, and the arrow red. Discuss how you start at the left side and end on the right side of each word. Slide your finger down each arrow as you say the word. Place each word in the *Slide and Say* pocket. Pull it out one letter at a time and say each sound. Then, blend the word. Check if you said it correctly by revealing the picture. Place the word card on the race track. Place the race car over the beginning of the word and push it from the left to the checkered flag at the right as you blend and say the word.

9. Store the cards in the *Slide and Say* pocket. If desired, add more words using index cards cut in half length-wise.

## Reflect on Learning

To complete the left-hand page, say several segmented words. Have students record the word and blend it. For example, say /m/ /o/ /p/. Students should write and say *mop*. Then, challenge students to listen to a word and segment the sounds they hear. For example, say *pet*. Students should write *p*, *e*, and *t*.

© Carson-Dellosa • CD-104946

# Blending Sounds

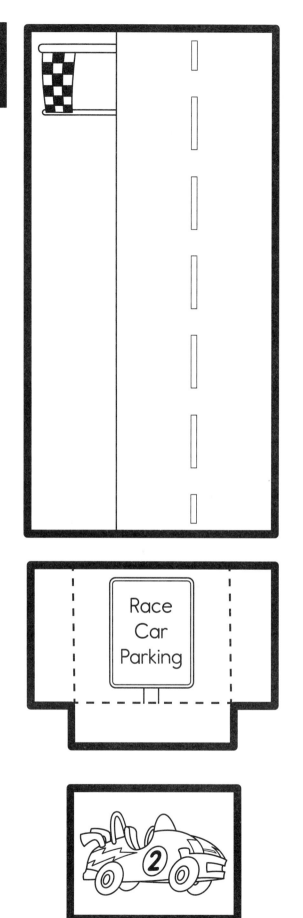

© Carson-Dellosa • CD-104946

# Understanding Syllables

## Introduction

Provide each student with a sheet of paper with a rectangle divided into three spaces horizontally. Then, distribute three counters, buttons, coins, or other small markers to each student. Explain that words can be broken into parts. Words can have one part, such as *dot, bed,* or *fish* or they can have more parts, such as *happy, apron, blueberry,* or *alligator.* As you say the words, emphasize and count the parts by marking tallies on the board or holding up fingers. Challenge students to listen and find the word parts. Say several words. For each word, have students place a marker in one of the sections on their paper for each part they hear. Repeat each word several times and then review it to check for any misconceptions.

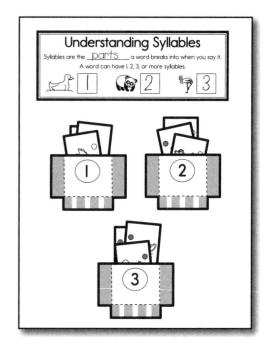

## Creating the Notebook Page

Guide students through the following steps to complete the right-hand page in their notebooks.

1.  Add a Table of Contents entry for the Understanding Syllables pages.

2.  Cut out the title and glue it to the top of the page.

3.  Complete the explanation (Syllables are the **parts** a word breaks into when you say it.) Say each example word and write the number of syllables it has in the box beside it.

4.  Cut out the three pockets. Apply glue to the backs of the three tabs and attach the pockets to the page below the title, leaving space between each one. It may be helpful to fold on the dashed lines to create visual borders before applying the glue.

5.  Cut out the picture cards.

6.  Say the name of the animal on each card. Color the dots to match the number of syllables in the word. Then, place the card in the correct pocket.

## Reflect on Learning

To complete the left-hand page, provide each student with three self-stick notes. Have students write *1, 2,* and *3* on the notes. Then, students should take a tour of the classroom and place each self-stick note on an object that has one, two, or three syllables. Students should write or draw the three objects they found and label each word or drawing *1, 2,* or *3.* As a class, discuss the objects found and how many syllables they each have.

© Carson-Dellosa • CD-104946

# Understanding Syllables

Syllables are the _____ a word breaks into when you say it.
A word can have 1, 2, 3, or more syllables.

 [ ]    [ ]    [ ]

© Carson-Dellosa • CD-104946

# Counting Syllables

*Students will need a sharpened pencil and a paper clip to complete the spinner activity.*

## Introduction

Explain that there are several different ways to count the number of syllables in a word. Demonstrate each strategy with the same set of words. Students can jump or clap the syllables, tap their finger on their hand, or watch their mouth in a mirror (or watch a partner's mouth) and count how many times it opens. Have students practice the strategies using their first, middle, and last names to find out how many syllables each one has.

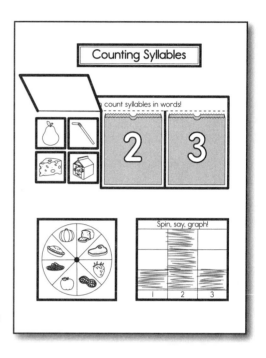

## Creating the Notebook Page

Guide students through the following steps to complete the right-hand page in their notebooks.

1.  Add a Table of Contents entry for the Counting Syllables pages.

2.  Cut out the title and glue it to the top of the page.

3.  Cut out the flap book. Cut on the solid lines to create three flaps. Apply glue to the back of the top section and attach it to the page below the title.

4.  Cut out the picture cards. Say the name of each food, count the syllables, and glue it under the matching paper bag flap. (Note: Some answers may differ; for example, cucumber (3) vs. pickle (2). Allow all answers as long as they can be explained.)

5.  Cut out the spinner and glue it to the bottom-left side of the page.

6.  Cut out the *Spin, say, graph!* piece and glue it to the right of the spinner.

7.  Use a sharpened pencil and a paper clip to create a spinner. Spin the spinner. Say the name of the picture it lands on, count the number of syllables in the word, and then add it to the graph in the correct column. Repeat several times to practice counting syllables in words.

## Reflect on Learning

To complete the left-hand page, have students cut pictures of several objects from a magazine. Then, students should sort the objects by the number of syllables each word has. They should glue the pictures in a group and label them with the number of syllables.

© Carson-Dellosa • CD-104946

# Counting Syllables

## I can count syllables in words!

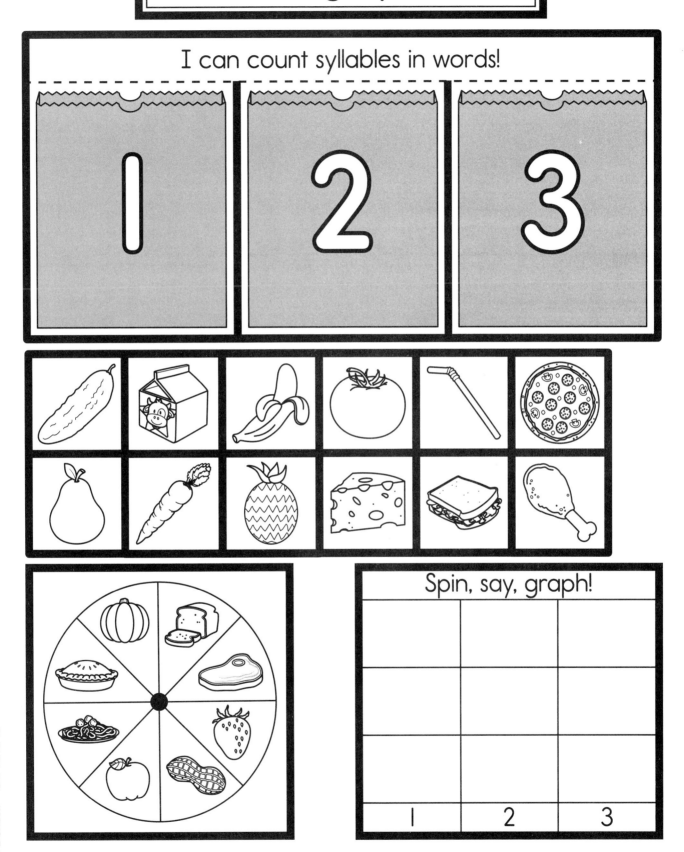

1

2

3

### Spin, say, graph!

| 1 | 2 | 3 |
|---|---|---|

© Carson-Dellosa • CD-104946

# Understanding Rhyming Words

## Introduction

Read a short rhyming poem aloud (for example, *I saw a little bee / Buzzing around near me. / I was as still as I could be / So he sat upon my knee.*). Have students identify the words that sound the same. (You may need to read it several times.) Record the words on the board. Explain that the words are rhyming words because they sound the same. Challenge students to identify which part of the words sounds the same (the end).

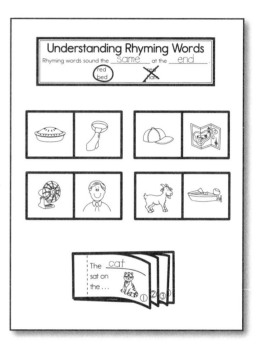

## Creating the Notebook Page

Guide students through the following steps to complete the right-hand page in their notebooks.

1.  Add a Table of Contents entry for the Understanding Rhyming Words pages.

2.  Cut out the title and glue it to the top of the page.

3.  Complete the explanation (Rhyming words sound the **same** at the **end**.) Look at the pairs of example words. Circle the set that rhymes. Cross out the set that does not rhyme.

4.  Cut out the picture cards.

5.  Say the name of the picture on each card and find the rhyming word. Glue each pair to the page below the title, leaving space at the bottom of the page.

6.  Cut out the four flaps. Apply glue to the gray glue sections and stack the flaps to create a stacked four-flap book. Use the page numbers to assemble the pages in the correct order. Glue the book to the bottom of the page.

7.  Read each page of the book. Use the pictures to fill in the blank with rhyming words (from front to back: **cat**, **rat**, **rat**, **hat**). On the last page, fill in the blank with a rhyming word of your choice and draw a picture to match.

## Reflect on Learning

To complete the left-hand page, write several simple words on the board, such as *pop*, *man*, and *fly*. Have students record each word in their notebook and try to come up with as many rhyming words for each word as they can.

© Carson-Dellosa • CD-104946

# Understanding Rhyming Words

Rhyming words sound the _____ at the _____ .

| red | red |
|-----|-----|
| bed | ham |

The _____
sat on
the . . .    1

_____ !
The _____
sat on the . . .    2

_____ !
I sat
on the . . .    3

_____ !
4

© Carson-Dellosa • CD-104946

# Finding Rhyming Words

## Introduction

Review rhyming words. Write four words that are easy to rhyme with on the board, such as *pat*, *be*, etc. Provide each student with a small piece of paper and have her write a word that rhymes with one of the four words on the board. Then, have all students walk around the room and find all of the other students that have a word that rhymes with theirs. Once all students have found their group, allow each group to share their rhyming words.

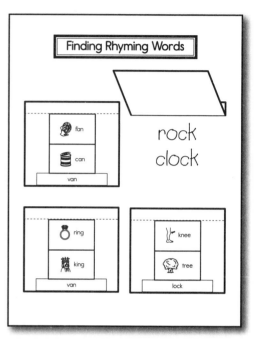

## Creating the Notebook Page

Guide students through the following steps to complete the right-hand page in their notebooks.

1. Add a Table of Contents entry for the Finding Rhyming Words pages.

2. Cut out the title and glue it to the top of the page.

3. Cut out the four hat flaps. Apply glue to the back of the top sections and attach them to the page.

4. Cut out the picture and word cards.

5. Say the word on each card and glue it to a space on the matching hat.

6. Under each flap, write more words that rhyme with the words on the hat.

## Reflect on Learning

To complete the left-hand page, provide students with a short, simple poem with several rhyming words to glue in their notebooks. Read the poem together. Then, have students highlight or circle the rhyming words they find. If there are different sets of rhyming words, have students use a different color to circle or highlight each set.

© Carson-Dellosa • CD-104946

# Finding Rhyming Words

block    fan    can    king

ring    sock    knee    tree

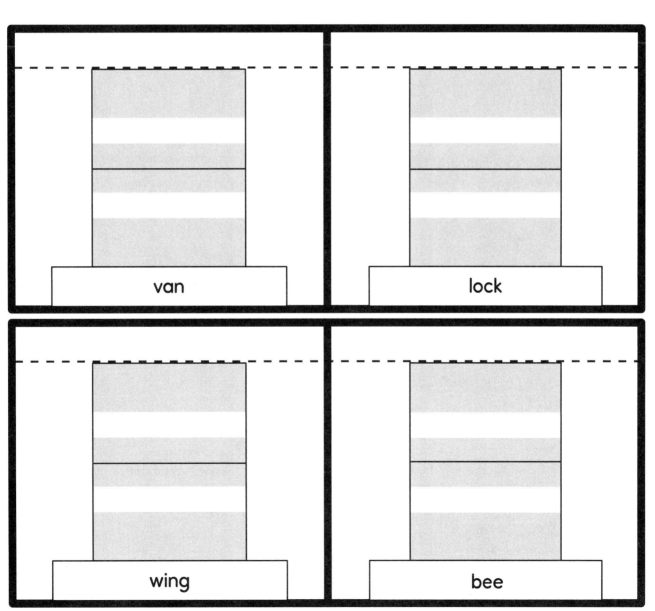

van

lock

wing

bee

© Carson-Dellosa • CD-104946

# Word Families

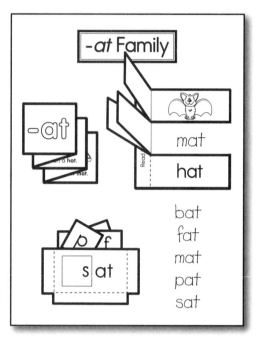

## Introduction

Review rhyming words. Display a poem with rhyming words. Make sure the rhyming words use the same spelling (for example, *dog*, *hog*, and *log*, not *bee*, *me*, and *sea*). Have students circle the rhyming words. Rewrite the rhyming words in a list. As a class, discuss how the rhyming words share the same ending. Then, challenge students to come up with more rhyming words. Explain that words with the same ending are part of a word family.

## Creating the Notebook Page

Guide students through the following steps to complete the right-hand page in their notebooks.

1.  Add a Table of Contents entry for the Word Families pages.

2.  Cut out the title and glue it to the top of the page.

3.  Cut out the accordion fold piece. With the word family name on top, fold back and forth on the dashed lines to create an accordion fold. Apply glue to the back of the piece and attach it to the top left of the page.

4.  Open the accordion fold and read the story. Identify the words in the word family.

5.  Cut out the two flap books. Cut on the solid lines to create three flaps on each. Apply glue to the gray glue section and place the other flap book on top to create a stacked six-flap book. Apply glue to the back of the left section and attach it to the right of the accordion fold book.

6.  On the flap book, read the word on the top flap, say it, and use the bottom flap to check if you said it right. Then, write the word under the bottom flap.

7.  Cut out the pocket. Apply glue to the backs of the three tabs and attach the pocket to the bottom-left side of the page. It may be helpful to have students fold on the dashed lines to create visual borders before applying the glue.

8.  Cut out the letter cards. Place each letter card in the box on the pocket to form a word. Say the word and write it on the page beside the pocket. Store the letters in the pocket.

9.  Use the blank template on page 75 to create pages for word families of your choosing.

## Reflect on Learning

To complete the left-hand page, provide students with a set of nonsense words from that word family to glue in their notebooks, or write them on the board for students to copy. Include one or two words that are not part of the word family. Students should cross out the words that are not part of the word family.

© Carson-Dellosa • CD-104946

on a **flat mat.**

He saw **that rat**

**sat** on a **hat.**

The **fat cat**

-at

Read it. Say it. Write it.

bat

mat

hat

glue

WELCOME

at

-at Family

b

f

m

p

s

© Carson-Dellosa • CD-104946

man

pan

ran

© Carson-Dellosa • CD-104946

-an Family

b

c

f

t

v

Read it. Say it. Write it.

glue

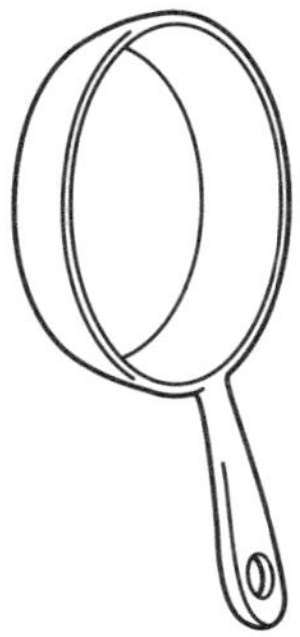

an

in the **tan van.**

He saw a **can** and **fan**

**ran** to a **tan van.**

A **man** named **Dan**

-an

**70** Word Families

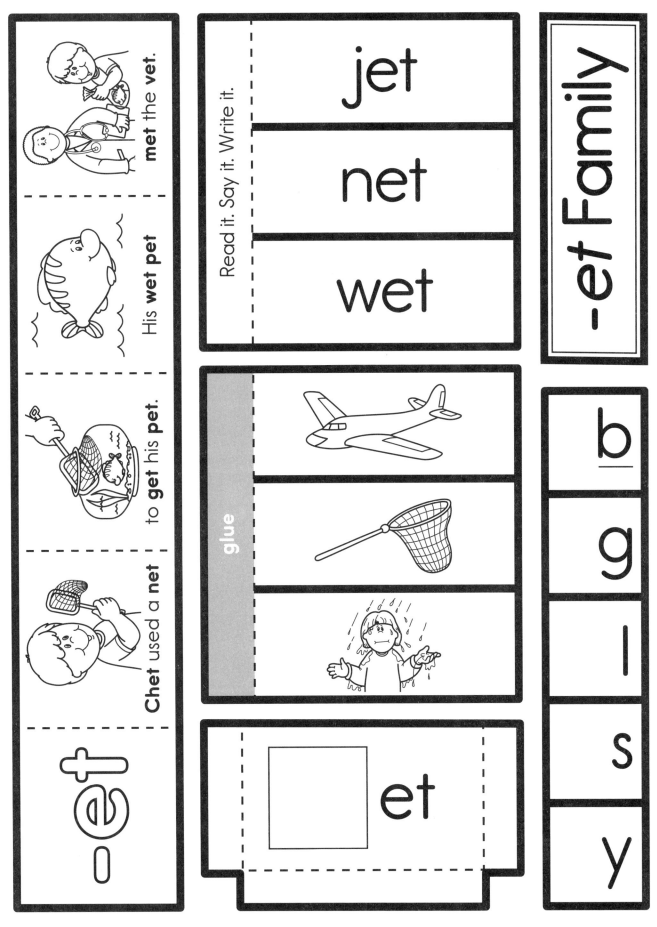

**-et Family**

jet

net

wet

Read it. Say it. Write it.

glue

et

met the vet.

His wet pet

to get his pet.

Chet used a net

-et

b

g

l

s

y

© Carson-Dellosa • CD-104946

and make his **twin grin.**

He likes to **win**

likes to **spin.**

A **twin** with a **fin**

-in

Read it. Say it. Write it.

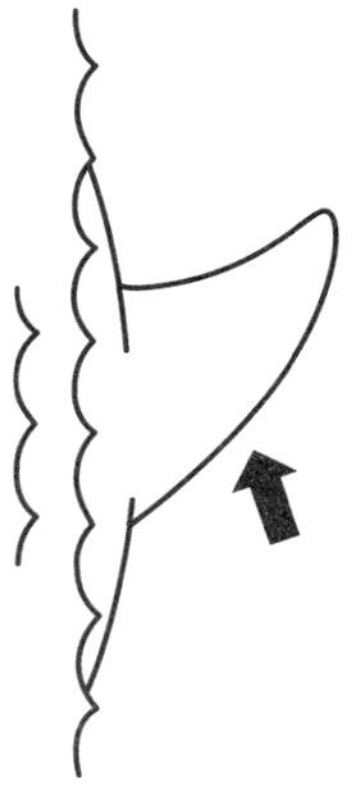

bin

fin

pin

glue

in

## -in Family

b

k

p

t

w

© Carson-Dellosa • CD-104946

**-og Family**

Read it. Say it. Write it.

dog

hog

log

glue

og

b

c

f

j

l

jog by the **log**.

They saw a **frog**

sat by a **bog**.

A **dog** and a **hog**

og

© Carson-Dellosa • CD-104946

# -ug Family

Read it. Say it. Write it.

bug

mug

rug

glue

ug

d

h

j

t

-ug

and a **jug** to the **rug**.

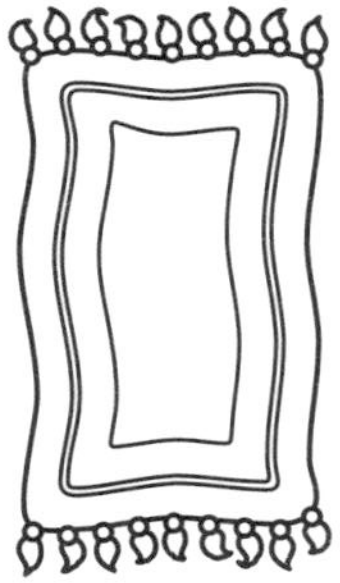

A **slug** took a **mug**.

played **tug** on a **rug**.

A **bug** and a **pug**.

© Carson-Dellosa • CD-104946

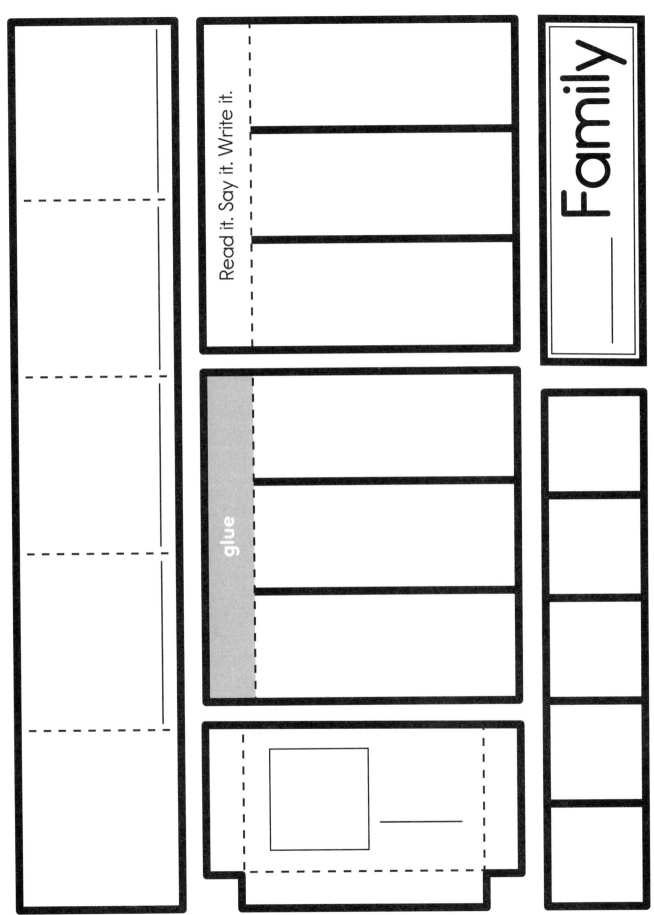

Read it. Say it. Write it.

glue

Family

© Carson-Dellosa • CD-104946

# Adding -s or -es

© Carson-Dellosa • CD-104946

## Introduction

In one hand, hold an object, such as a button, sheet of paper, card, ball, etc. Tell the class, *I have one button* as you hold up that object. Then pick up more and say, *I have many buttons*. Write the words *button* and *buttons* on the board. Give several more examples on the board. Explain that when you are talking or writing about more than one object, you add an /s/ sound to the word. If desired, introduce the word *plural*.

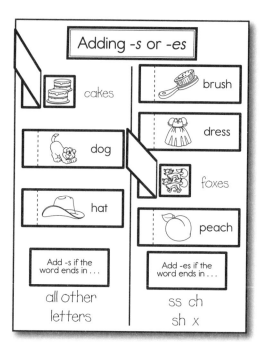

## Creating the Notebook Page

Guide students through the following steps to complete the right-hand page in their notebooks.

1. Add a Table of Contents entry for the Adding -s or -es pages.

2. Cut out the title and glue it to the top of the page.

3. Cut out the flaps.

4. Say the word on each flap. Then, say the plural form. Discuss the two different sounds the words need (*s* and *es*). Sort the flaps into two piles, depending on which sound they need.

5. Apply glue to the back of the left section of each flap and glue them to the page, creating a column for each sorted pile. Leave space below each set. If desired, draw a line between the columns.

6. Cut out the picture cards. Glue them under the matching flap, leaving space beside each picture to write a word.

7. Discuss how you add an -s to some words and add an -es to other words to make them plural. Write the plural form of each word under the flap.

8. Cut out the rule pieces. Glue each one under the correct set of words.

9. Identify the endings of the -es words and use them to complete the rule (**-ss**, **-ch**, **-sh**, and **-x**). If desired, underline or highlight the ending on each flap. Then, complete the rule for the -s words (**all other letters**).

## Reflect on Learning

To complete the left-hand page, write several words on the board. Have students write the plural of each word. If the word ends in -es, students should circle the part of the word that changes the ending.

brush

dress

fox

peach

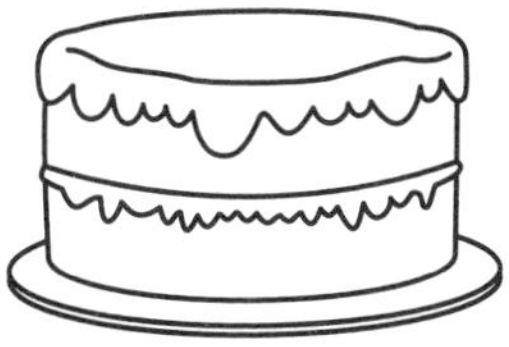

cake

dog

hat

**Adding -s or -es**

Add -s if the
word ends in . . .

Add -es if the
word ends in . . .

© Carson-Dellosa • CD-104946

# Tabs

Cut out each tab and label it. Apply glue to the back of each tab and align it on the outside edge of the page with only the label section showing beyond the edge. Then, fold each tab to seal the page inside.

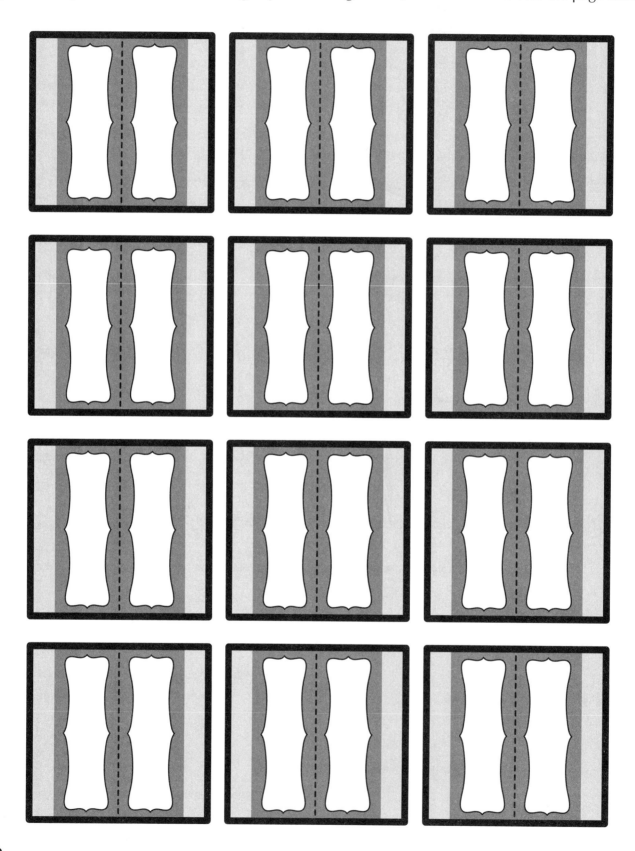

© Carson-Dellosa • CD-104946

## KWL Chart

Cut out the KWL chart and cut on the solid lines to create three separate flaps. Apply glue to the back of the Topic section to attach the chart to a notebook page.

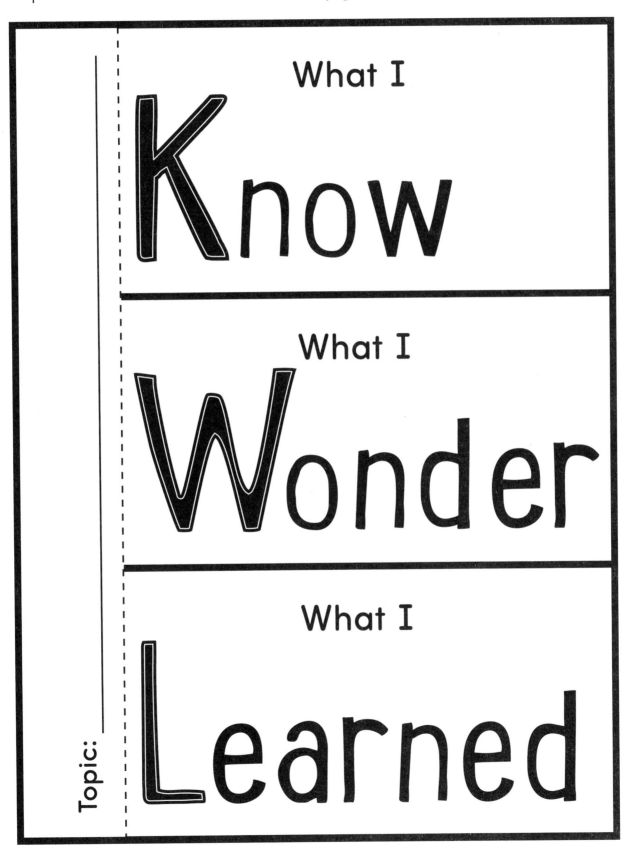

© Carson-Dellosa • CD-104946

# Library Pocket

Cut out the library pocket on the solid lines. Fold in the side tabs and apply glue to them before folding up the front of the pocket. Apply glue to the back of the pocket to attach it to a notebook page.

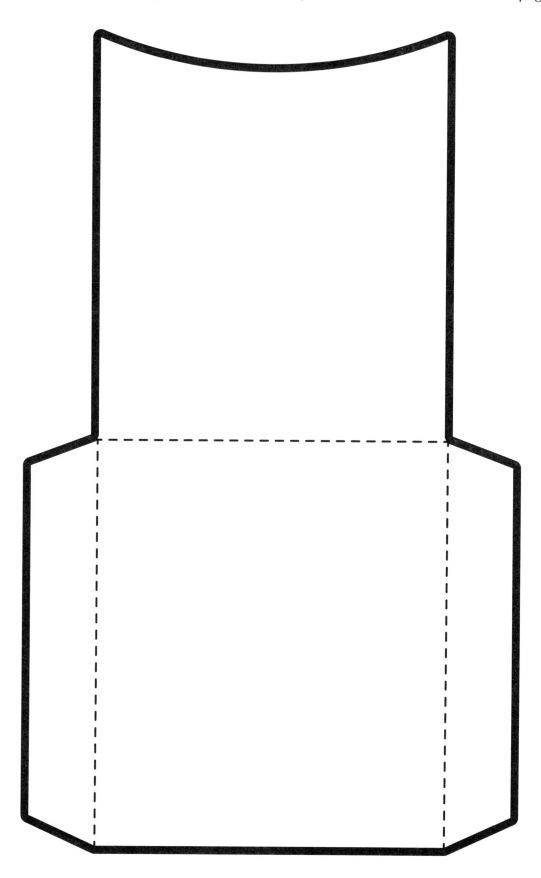

© Carson-Dellosa • CD-104946

# Envelope

Cut out the envelope on the solid lines. Fold in the side tabs and apply glue to them before folding up the rectangular front of the envelope. Fold down the triangular flap to close the envelope. Apply glue to the back of the envelope to attach it to a notebook page.

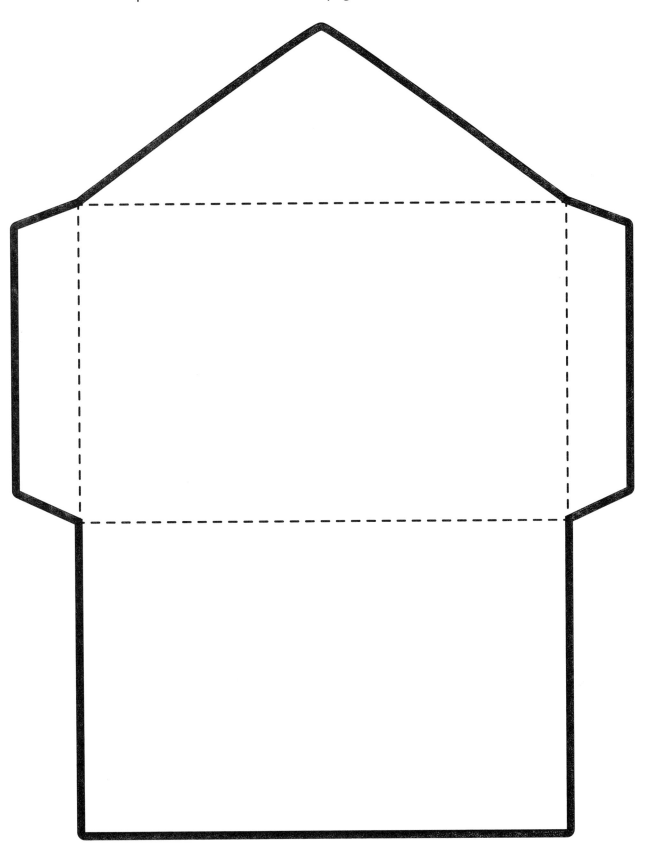

© Carson-Dellosa • CD-104946

# Pocket and Cards

Cut out the pocket on the solid lines. Fold over the front of the pocket. Then, apply glue to the tabs and fold them around the back of the pocket. Apply glue to the back of the pocket to attach it to a notebook page. Cut out the cards and store them in the envelope.

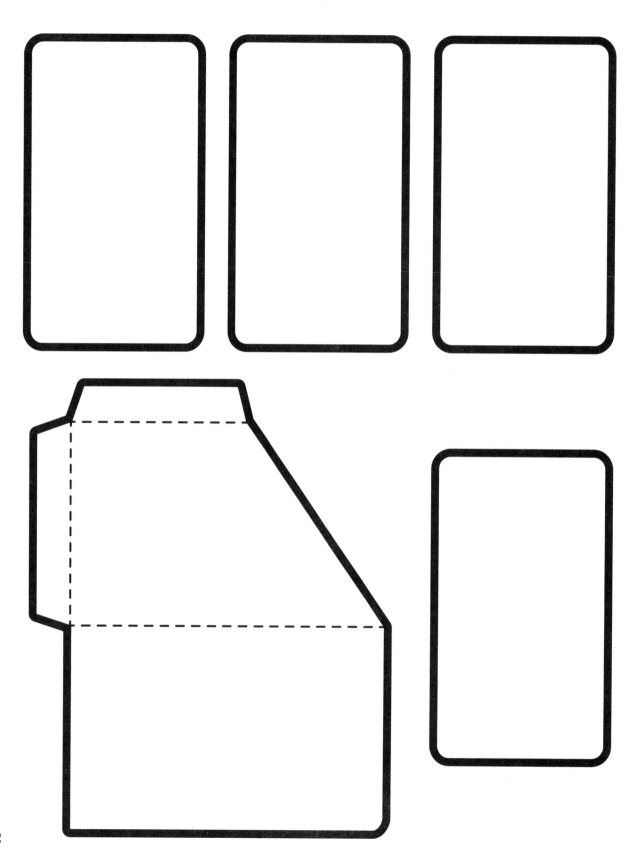

© Carson-Dellosa • CD-104946

# Six-Flap Shutter Fold

Cut out the shutter fold around the outside border. Then, cut on the solid lines to create six flaps. Fold the flaps toward the center. Apply glue to the back of the shutter fold to attach it to a notebook page.

If desired, this template can be modified to create a four-flap shutter fold by cutting off the bottom row. You can also create two three-flap books by cutting it in half down the center line.

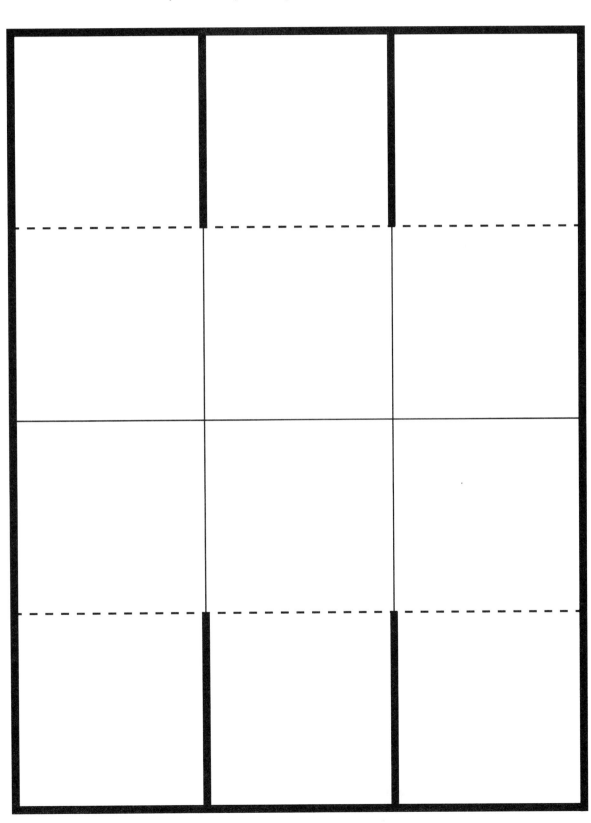

© Carson-Dellosa • CD-104946

# Eight-Flap Shutter Fold

Cut out the shutter fold around the outside border. Then, cut on the solid lines to create eight flaps. Fold the flaps toward the center. Apply glue to the back of the shutter fold to attach it to a notebook page.

If desired, this template can be modified to create two four-flap shutter folds by cutting off the bottom two rows. You can also create two four-flap books by cutting it in half down the center line.

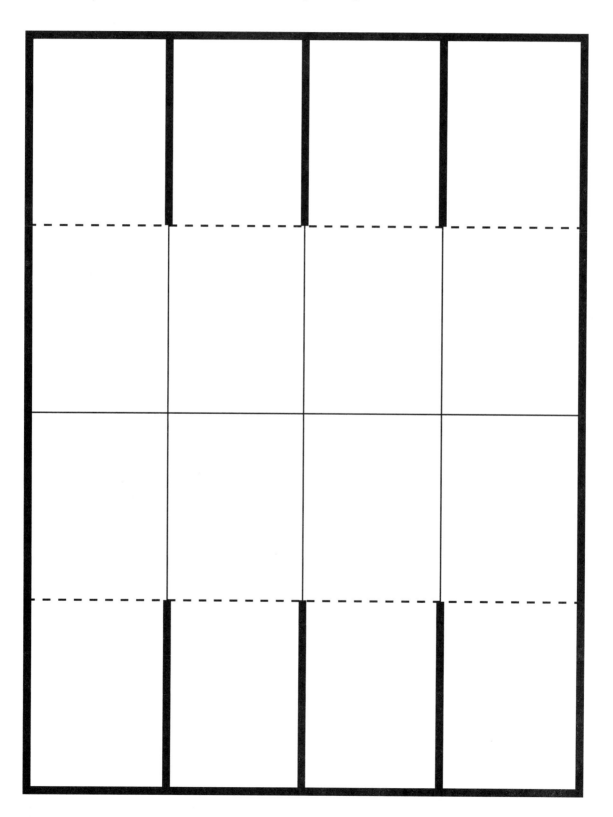

© Carson-Dellosa • CD-104946

# Flap Book—Eight Flaps

Cut out the flap book around the outside border. Then, cut on the solid lines to create eight flaps. Apply glue to the back of the center section to attach it to a notebook page.

If desired, this template can be modified to create a six-flap or two four-flap books by cutting off the bottom row or two. You can also create a tall four-flap book by cutting off the flaps on the left side.

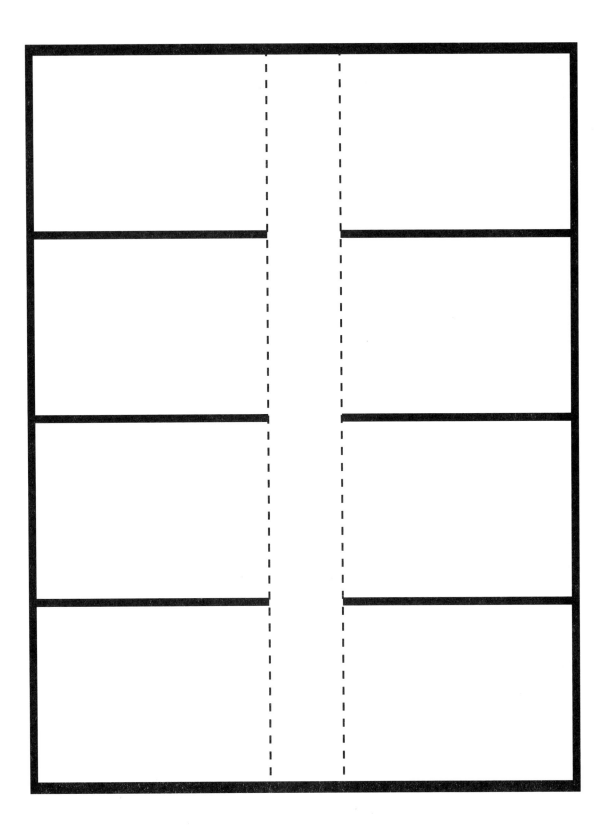

© Carson-Dellosa • CD-104946

# Flap Book—Twelve Flaps

Cut out the flap book around the outside border. Then, cut on the solid lines to create 12 flaps. Apply glue to the back of the center section to attach it to a notebook page.

If desired, this template can be modified to create smaller flap books by cutting off any number of rows from the bottom. You can also create a tall flap book by cutting off the flaps on the left side.

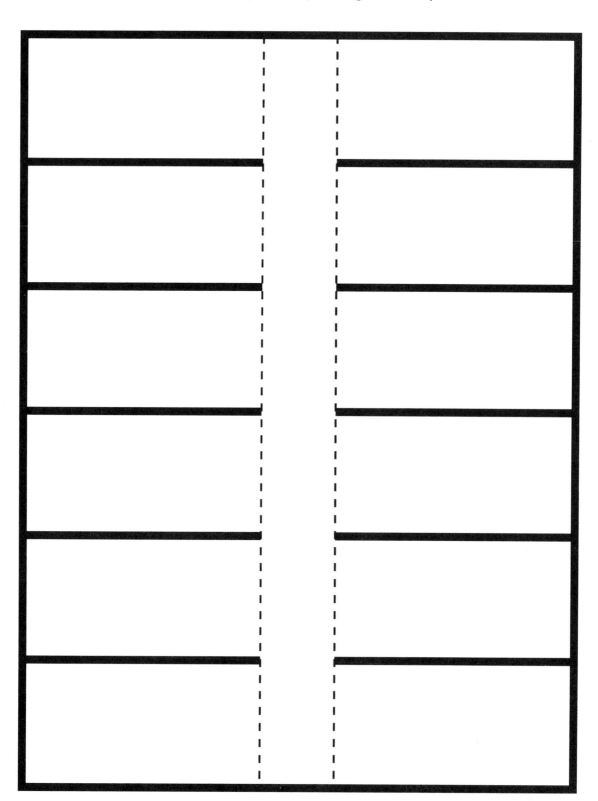

© Carson-Dellosa • CD-104946

# Shaped Flaps

Cut out each shaped flap. Apply glue to the back of the narrow section to attach it to a notebook page.

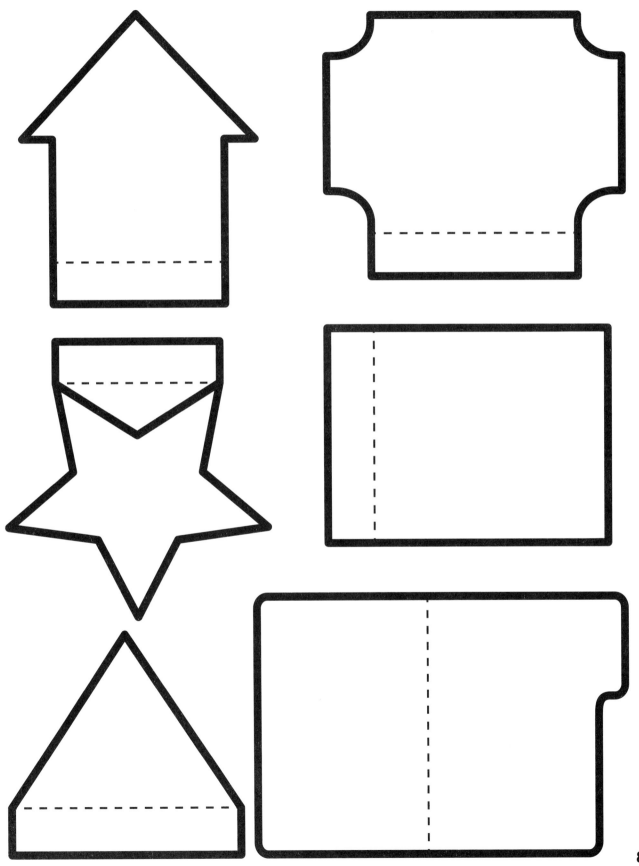

© Carson-Dellosa • CD-104946

# Shaped Flaps

© Carson-Dellosa • CD-104946

# Interlocking Booklet

Cut out the booklet on the solid lines, including the short vertical lines on the top and bottom flaps. Then, fold the top and bottom flaps toward the center, interlocking them using the small vertical cuts. Apply glue to the back of the center panel to attach it to a notebook page.

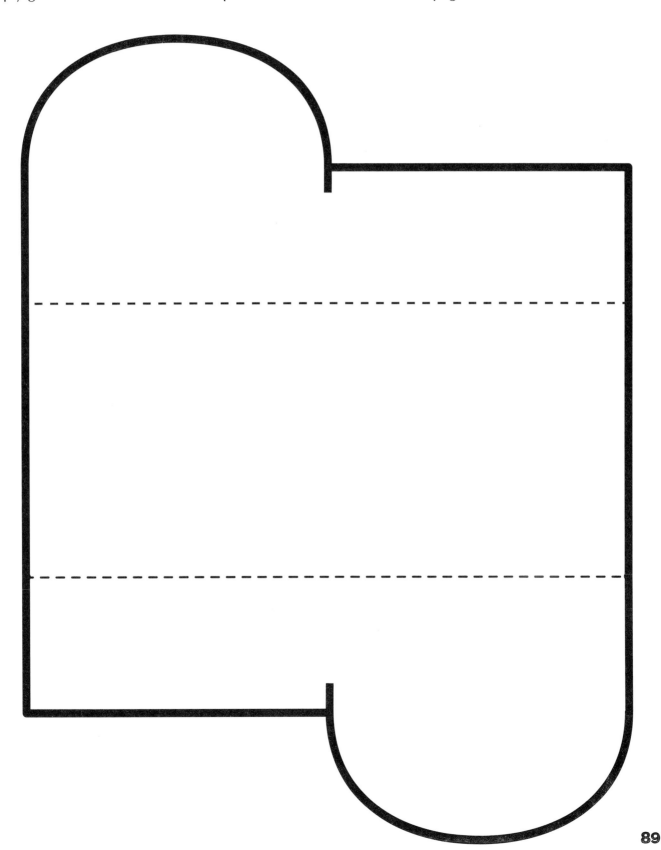

© Carson-Dellosa • CD-104946

# Four-Flap Petal Fold

Cut out the shape on the solid lines. Then, fold the flaps toward the center. Apply glue to the back of the center panel to attach it to a notebook page.

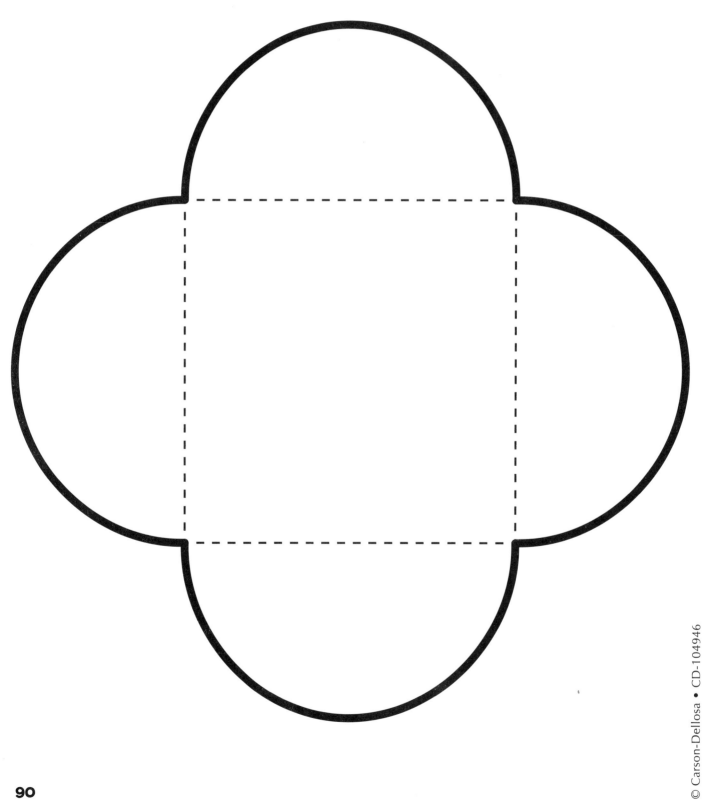

© Carson-Dellosa • CD-104946

# Six-Flap Petal Fold

Cut out the shape on the solid lines. Then, fold the flaps toward the center and back out. Apply glue to the back of the center panel to attach it to a notebook page.

© Carson-Dellosa • CD-104946

# Accordion Folds

Cut out the accordion pieces on the solid lines. Fold on the dashed lines, alternating the fold direction. Apply glue to the back of the last section to attach it to a notebook page.

You may modify the accordion books to have more or fewer pages by cutting off extra pages or by having students glue the first and last panels of two accordion books together.

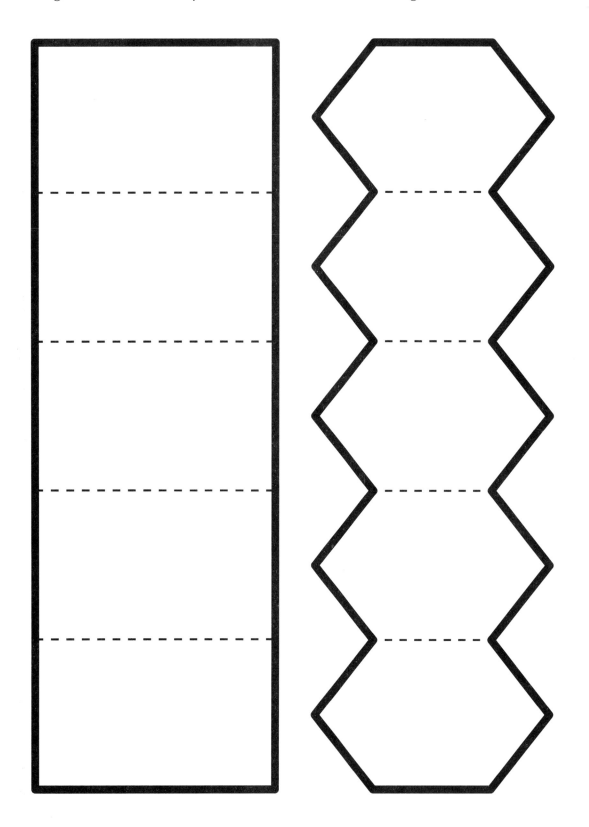

© Carson-Dellosa • CD-104946

# Accordion Folds

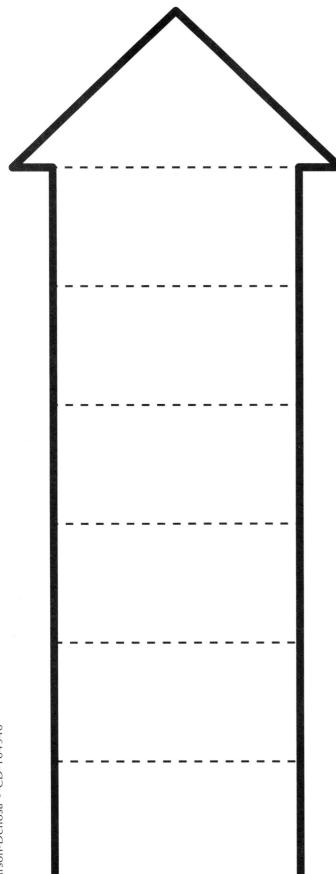

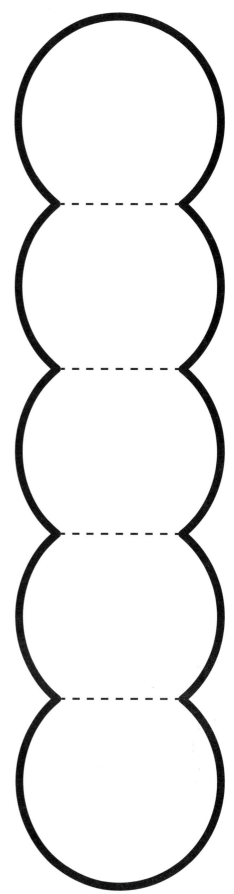

© Carson-Dellosa • CD-104946

# Clamshell Fold

Cut out the clamshell fold on the solid lines. Fold and unfold the piece on the three dashed lines. With the piece oriented so that the folds form an X with a horizontal line through it, pull the left and right sides together at the fold line. Then, keeping the sides touching, bring the top edge down to meet the bottom edge. You should be left with a triangular shape that unfolds into a square. Apply glue to the back of the triangle to attach the clamshell to a notebook page.

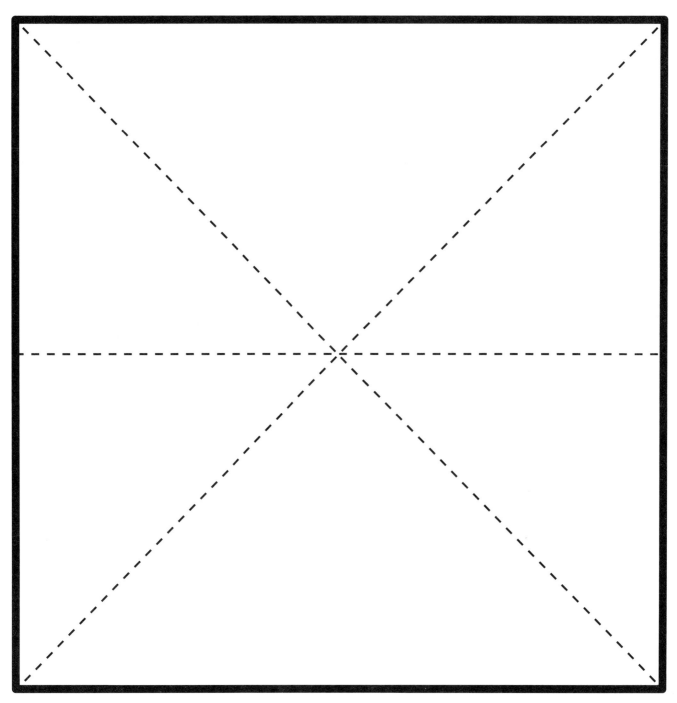

© Carson-Dellosa • CD-104946

# Puzzle Pieces

Cut out each puzzle along the solid lines to create a three- or four-piece puzzle. Apply glue to the back of each puzzle piece to attach it to a notebook page. Alternatively, apply glue only to one edge of each piece to create flaps.

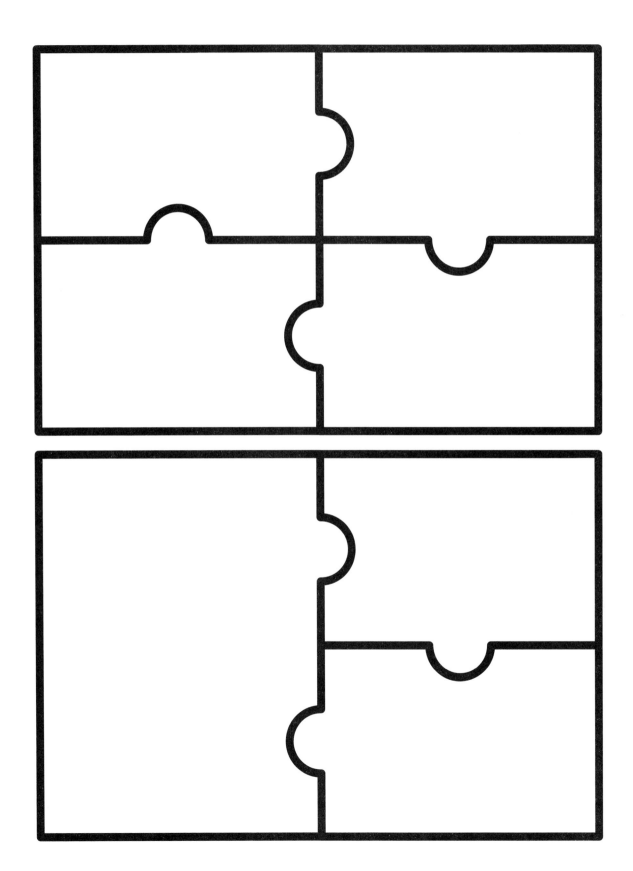

© Carson-Dellosa • CD-104946

# Flip Book

Cut out the two rectangular pieces on the solid lines. Fold each rectangle on the dashed lines. Fold the first piece so the gray glue section is inside the fold. Apply glue to the gray glue section and place the other folded rectangle on top so that the folds are nested and create a book with four cascading flaps. Make sure that the inside pages are facing up so that the edges of both pages are visible. Apply glue to the back of the book to attach it to a notebook page.

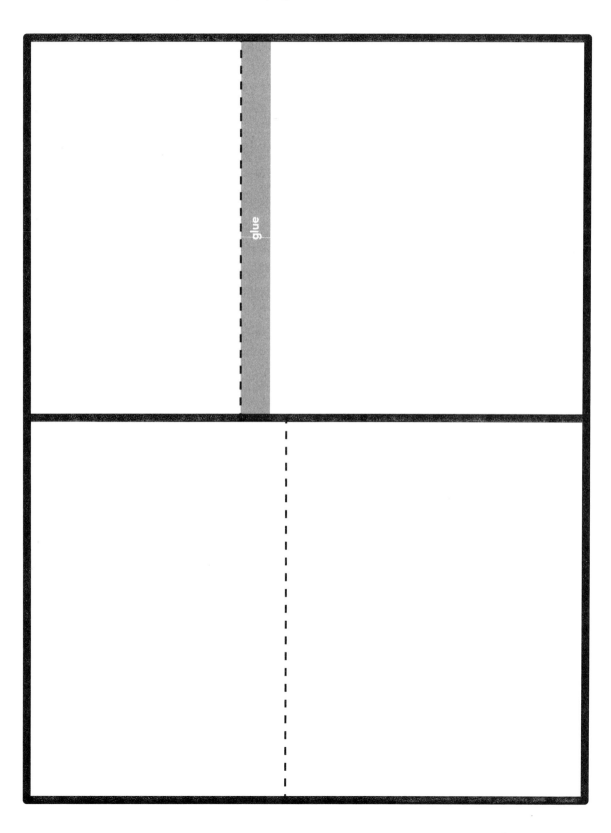

glue

© Carson-Dellosa • CD-104946